Shenomenal
W♡men

Shenomenal Women

WOMEN WHO GAVE UP EXCUSES AND MADE A WAY THROUGH LIFE'S MOST CHALLENGING TIMES

TASHA CHAMPION

purposely
created
PUBLISHING

Special discounts are available on bulk quantity purchases by book clubs, associations and special interest groups. For details email: sales@publishyourgift.com or call (888) 949-6228.
For information log on to www.PublishYourGift.com

This book is dedicated to the women who find encouragement through the stories so honestly shared in each chapter.

If you found strength to overcome obstacles, may you continue to soar through your path of healing. This book honors you for stepping out of your comfort zone and discovering your way out, to emerge a woman who knows her value is not dictated by her past.

If you are currently going through obstacles, may you recognize you have the power within you to change your circumstances. This book honors the fighter in you who is not giving up because you know your worth is defined by you and not your situation.

Wherever you are in life, acknowledge where you are on your journey, speak and own your truth, trust God (or whatever your higher power is), and know you are worthy of healing and living your best life. Whether you've overcome or are currently going through a battle, you, along with the beautiful women in this book, are a Shenomenal Woman!

Table of Contents

Acknowledgments

I am so appreciative of the support I have received during the journey of my healing. I never know how God will use me, so I remain open to whatever He has for me. Sitting at my desk on April 29, 2020, I felt God say, "You're going to write an anthology book called *Shenomenal Women*."

"Who's writing a book?" I responded.

"You are."

Knowing that I can sometimes procrastinate, God took my hand and kicked my actions into high gear. He didn't slow me down until *everything* was in order. Everyone that I am acknowledging has played a major role in my journey, which resulted in the creation of this book.

My babies, my world, my children, my fantastic four. There will never be enough words to express my love for you. The four of you give me the strength I need to endure any challenge. You guys trusted me, even when I failed you. You believed in me when I didn't believe in myself. The support I'm always shown from you is unmatched. There is so much more to come from us as a family and each of you individually. We are the Champions, and the world will know that we have championed through every storm that came our way with love in our hearts and a smile on our face.

My mom, Priscilla Roberts, and my aunts, Valerie Curry and Traci Hoyd. You three have encouraged me and prayed for me through every battle. Whenever I felt alone or misunderstood, you were there in my corner giving me guidance. I appreciate the talks, the love, the support, and most of all, the truth and wisdom. Thank you for being significant in my growth. You have defined Shenomenal for me!

My natural sister, Tish Smith, and my spiritual sister/cousin, Bianca Page. The rebirth and growth of our relationships have been heartfelt. Tish, being diagnosed with breast cancer two weeks apart, we became survivors together. Bianca, we have pushed each other and had many spiritual awakening conversations. You both serve major parts of my life and journey that has led me here.

My GOI (God of Israel) church family. Everything I do, you guys show up and show out to support and pray me through it. I know I have an incredible foundation of organic and genuine love through spirit to guide me because of each of you.

Elyse Falzone, my life coach. When God sent you to me, I was completely broken. You showed me how to put the pieces of me back together so my life could come together. You taught me that my truth, my spirit, and my intuitiveness were my God-given gifts to honor and to use in helping others. Through my work with you, I discovered who I was and learned to love myself. I found my authentic and genuine smile, and my life was forever changed.

To Kiana Shaw, visionary author of *A Mother's Diary*, the first book I was a part of, thank you for allowing me to be your confidant during the journey of that book. Little did I know God put me in that position to prepare me for this.

Shiela Thompson, you gave me Shenomenal in 2017 from my very first workshop. When you spoke the word, my spirit grabbed it and held it. I knew it was a special word but never knew God would guide me to using it for the title of this book.

To my extended family and friends. Thank you for your unwavering love and support.

Finally, to my Shenomenal co-authors. Thank you for trusting me and enduring this journey with me. You answered the assignment God gave you when you said yes. This is your time as much as it is mine. We shared our struggles and tears, and each of us kept going. People are reading this book right now because of each of you. I am honored and in awe of your honesty and willingness to inspire others from your own experiences. I love you all.

Love and Light,
Tasha Champion

Foreword

Through a cancer diagnosis, Tasha's voice was developed.

She didn't have an illness that affected her voice. She just chose not to use it, not to speak up for herself, without regard to the strain it would put on her life.

Becoming a survivor awakened something inside of her to help people who have to hear that dreadful phrase, "You have cancer." Tasha became an integral part of the High Desert Cancer Connection, where she began to speak powerful words of encouragement for those fighting the disease. Through that work, she has been honored by multiple organizations and asked to be a guest speaker on many health platforms.

I have seen a natural love in my daughter to inspire others to find and live their best life. She strongly affirms that can only begin with their truth. As she started to live in her own truth, others around her started listening and receiving from her wisdom. Right before my eyes, the life coach in her was born. I am blessed to be a witness of the changes in my daughter's life. She is a self-motivator who decided to live her dreams out loud. Tasha refuses to allow any past experiences that were not conducive to her life to be present in her future. That life has included a divorce that left her to be a single mom 100 percent of the time to her four children. They are her biggest blessing and a product of her stern and loving rearing. She keeps them grounded and teaches them to love and appreciate life even through life's hardest moments.

Through everything that happens and all that she has been through, she makes a decision to live a positive, spiritual (not religious) life. Her faith in God through it all has heightened to a stance she refuses to let go of.

Tasha's passion in helping women heal, discover their truth, and live life on their terms came from her own struggles. Her pain, followed by her commitment to heal, led her to finding her voice and her purpose. This book is a work of her transparency and honesty shared with other inspirational women. When this project is complete, it will be a motivational and "Shenomenal" piece!

Love You,
Priscilla Roberts
Proud and Elated Mom

When the Fairy Tale Ends

ANN-MARIE ANDERSON

I met my knight in shining armor in November 1993 at the age of 19. We had a whirlwind romance, and by March, decided to get married. Like most well-intentioned family and friends, everyone warned us we were moving too fast and making a huge mistake. Determined to prove everyone wrong, we pressed full speed ahead. We knew it was meant to be. We were both at a crossroads, had a lot in common, wanted the same things in life, and were going to church. This had to be right. On Memorial Day Weekend in 1994, we were married. The ceremony was emotional and beautiful. As we stood at the altar, eyes full of love and hope, I thought to myself, "I have dreamt of this moment my whole life. We are going to live happily ever after just like every Disney movie. Unlike our parents, we will get this right. We know the mistakes they made, and we know how to avoid them." In fact, the words our pastor spoke echoed in my heart for years to come: "A three-strand cord is not easily broken; keep God at the center of your marriage always, no matter what storms come, and you will be fine." Nothing could have prepared me for what was to come.

In 1995, we received amazing news. We were expecting our first child. It wasn't planned, but we were still over the moon with excitement. In my second trimester, I started having a lot of medical complications and ended up being hospitalized for a couple weeks. Upon discharge from the hospital, I had to be rushed back later that evening only to find out I was in pre-term labor. I still remember the words of my OB/GYN as if it were yesterday. "You're in labor. You're dilated to 10. The baby is coming. Unfortunately, because you're only 20 weeks along, his lungs aren't fully developed, and we won't be able to save him. I'm sorry." My heart sank as the tears quietly rolled down the side of my cheeks. I can still feel the chill that came over me. A hush lingered in the room as he instructed the nurse to turn off the monitor. He also told us I had an incompetent cervix and would not be able to carry a baby to term without having surgery. I had questions, but my mind could only think about the fact I would never hear my baby's heartbeat again. After five hours of labor, my baby boy, Bryson Keith, was born. He was so still, so quiet, and the moment most parents look forward to was suddenly dark and painful. My heart was so broken. I couldn't even hold him, but he was perfect; 10 tiny fingers, 10 tiny toes, and perfectly shaped lips. This was our first storm.

In the coming weeks and months, we cried and prayed together but never took time to heal individually as parents or as a couple. Life just kept going. Growing up in a home that did not foster self-expression, vulnerability, or any semblance of weakness, I didn't know where to put my pain. I tucked it away and kept busy with work and ministry. I don't believe either of us was equipped with the necessary tools to deal with the loss. However, by the grace of God and with a lot of prayers, we weathered this storm. About nine months later, we received news that we were expecting again.

We were both excited and terrified. This time we were more prepared. I had an amazing high-risk OB/GYN who happened to share our last name. I don't know if that was God's way of reassuring me, but I saw it as a hidden blessing. He took great care of us, and at 12 weeks of pregnancy, I had surgery to have a cervical cerclage placed to keep my cervix from opening too soon, increasing my chances of carrying my baby to full term. I was placed on bed rest for most of my pregnancy after that. A few months later, our perfect beautiful little girl made her debut into the world. This time, the cries that filled the room were the most amazing tones I'd ever heard. The room was filled with so much joy and laughter. Of course, I thought of Bryson and felt a longing in my heart, but in that moment, all was right in our world. I knew God had felt my pain, heard my cries, and seen my tears. Four years later, we welcomed our second perfect little angel. Although I still had the cervical cerclage, this was my easiest pregnancy, and quiet as it's kept, my easiest child.

In 2001, an unexpected pregnancy was welcomed news. My son was born in August 2002. Perfectly pink, like his sisters, all fingers, and all toes, but this time, it was different. No crying. I didn't get to hold him. "He's a little depressed," the doctor told my husband. "We're going to take him to NICU for monitoring." They found out he had an infection and began treating him with antibiotics.

We visited him in the NICU. Unable to touch him, it was clear that we were leaving the hospital without our baby. The storm of emotions began to brew inside of me. Fear started to come over me. I was immediately back in the hospital with my first son, who didn't make it, and we were terrified. I fell across my hospital bed and cried out to God "Why?" Heartbroken but hopeful, I went home without my baby. We visited every day, and a little after a week, we received a cryptic call urging us to come immediately. The doctor advised that our son had some sort of heart condition and that they were not equipped to care for him. The situation was dire, and they were transferring him to a children's hospital. When we saw him, I was shocked by his appearance. He was a grey color, and his face was sunken in like a malnourished child. Not the baby I left the night before. I could not understand why this was happening. It was not fair!

Our son had a rare heart condition, it wouldn't get better, and there wasn't a treatment. The only option was a heart transplant. I cried out again, "Lord, I can't do this again, and I'm not as strong as you think I am!" He said, "Yes you are. I keep my promises, and I won't leave you." I didn't believe it, but I just kept praying and fasting. I needed strength. I had two children to care for, a job, and a home to take care of. I didn't feel prepared to endure the storm at hand, but somehow God gave me just enough strength and grace for each day, and I was reminded that I was strong because God had me and He was faithful. I knew I couldn't quit.

The next few weeks seemed like I was walking in quicksand. Then a glimmer of hope. We walked into the hospital, and the doctor said, "I don't know what you guys are doing, but keep doing it. We did an echo-cardiogram on your son today and were surprised by the findings. We were so shocked that we did it three times. Your son has a different heart; it is not the same heart he came in here with." All we can say is that it was divine intervention! My son got a heart transplant, but he didn't need surgery. We sat there rejoicing, grateful as the storm inside of me began to calm. He would go on to live a life without one heart problem. God reminded me who He was and what I was made of. He showed me how to press through the fire. We survived another storm, but another one was on the horizon.

The same year my son was born, my husband lost his brother and his nephew. This man whom I thought hung the moon, my knight in shining armor, became someone I no longer recognized. I knew he was hurting, and I wanted to help, but I didn't know what to do. Unknown to me, he turned to alcohol, porn, and other vices to drown his pain. He kept me in the dark for several years, but gradually I noticed mood and behavior changes. I found email addresses, dating sites, and illicit messages to women on the computer, but I tried to ignore them. I didn't want to believe that he would ever do anything to hurt me. His drinking got worse, and he became verbally and somewhat physically abusive when he was intoxicated. This went on for several more years. He would forget to turn off his laptop, and I would find explicit communication between him and other women. There were unexplained lengthy calls at odd hours on the cell phone bill and social media messages from exes and other women with whom he was flirting. When I would confront him, he would tell me it was nothing. "It's just talk. I'm not doing anything," he would say.

In 2014, I found out he was having an affair and had been for nine months. He had taken her on business trips and spent days off with her when I thought he was working. To say I was devastated is a gross understatement. I wanted to leave him but didn't know how. I had been with him pretty much all my adult life. It was all I knew. It's interesting, growing up, I would always say if a man ever cheated on me, I was out of there. I would not tolerate that. Well, it was easier said than done. He said he would end things with her, and I decided to stay. He was my husband, and we had a family, a life together. I needed to believe him.

We decided to go to counseling and make it work. That was short lived. I recall planning a white party for his birthday that year. On the day of the party, I had a hair appointment and ended up taking his car. His work phone was in the car, and a text message came through. It was from his mistress with whom he was supposed to have ended things months before. She knew all about the party and was wishing him well and making plans to see him after. I was so angry! In that moment, I wanted to call off the party, but guests were coming and a lot of money had been spent. We argued when I got home, and he again claimed things were over with her and had no idea why she was texting. I didn't believe him, but it didn't matter because I had a party to host for a man who had again betrayed me and hurt me in ways I could not have imagined. I put on a bright smile and brave front and hosted an amazing party all while screaming inside. In the months to come, he would disappear in the middle of the night and then days at a time. I was at a loss but I decided to focus on God and the things over which I had control. I still had to work and take care of myself and my kids.

When you're in pain, you just need everything to pause and give you time, but life isn't that way. There were days when I didn't know if I could make it. Sometimes I went to work with no sleep. I kept leading worship at church and helping to lead other ministries. I'm telling you, God will be your strength when you have none left. In the natural it didn't seem possible, yet I made it through one day at a time all the while praying for my husband to change and shielding my kids from this person he had become. I was willing to do anything to keep my family together. I thought that's what I was supposed to do. Things did not get better, and if I saw a glimmer of hope, it was short lived. He did just about everything you could think of, and I died a little more inside each time. I didn't even know who I was any more. I had been his wife, my children's mom, a sister, and a daughter, but who was I without the titles? Who was Ann-Marie as an individual?

Everyone gets to a breaking point, and each time something happened, I became more and more numb to the idea of working it out. The final straw was Christmas Eve 2018. In a drunken rage, he punched me in my mouth. My youngest daughter called 911, and he was arrested. Instead of our traditional Christmas Eve discussing the birth of Christ, we were left with a shattered reality of the facade that had become our family. I'm sure he expected to come home and plead his case and that we start over *again*. Not this time. Apologize, forgive, repeat had become the broken record in my life with my husband. I was done playing that tune.

Over the next nine months, things continued to unfold that forced me to self-assess and made me realize I could no longer live this way. I had been repeatedly betrayed. I had put myself on the back burner for years, but no more. I wanted to recognize the person staring back at me in the mirror and get to know who she is. I needed to be strong enough to leave for good for myself, to show my daughters that it's okay to leave when something is toxic, and to show my son that a woman is to be cherished and protected. Sometimes I think I stayed too long, but then I remember God's timing is perfect.

When I dreamed of my wedding as a child, I didn't dream of my marriage. In the fairy tale, they stop at the beautiful wedding. They don't show the storms you will endure, the loss you will suffer, or the heartaches you feel you'll never recover from. While the princess walked off into the sunset with her prince, my knight in shining armor became a nightmare who presented pain instead of protection. No one ever explained that could happen.

I've had to do a lot of self-reflecting and a lot of inner healing. Through navigating this process, I'm getting to know this 47-year-old woman, and you know what? I love her. She is strong, fearless, and fierce with flaws and all but still standing in God's grace.

I choose to be in peace, living life on my terms, and I am worthy of it. Maybe I did get my fairytale ending, because choosing me is my happily ever after.

Heal the Little Girl Within

BIANCA A. PAGE, JD

In order to understand the woman I am now, I need to take you back to the root of my story where the fractures first began at ten years old. You see, I was a woman who lived by five toxic tenets, which created toxic relationships and a toxic identity that left me with no choice but to heal. On my journey, I realized that I had to reconnect with the little girl inside of me—the ten-year-old girl who had her heart broken, her world shattered, and her sense of security snatched away in an instant. I had to go back and heal her, love on her, and comfort her back to whole. I realized I was a toxic adult because I was still operating like a hurt ten-year-old girl who stopped playing, dreaming, loving, and living. In restoring little Bianca's innocence, I gave the adult Bianca permission to be a woman who is happy, healthy, whole, and complete.

THE BACKSTORY
I came from a loving family with an amazingly gifted mother, a nurturing and talented father, and a baby sister whom I adored. Our family unit felt safe and stable, and I felt protected. Whether we were living in a penthouse apartment in Michigan or struggling in a one-bedroom

apartment in Los Angeles, I was happy and "snug as a bug in a rug."

My parents ensured I went to private schools in the elite Baldwin Hills and Windsor Hills areas. The other families were unaware that I was a little girl from across the tracks with the youngest parents of the group. Mom and Dad always kept my uniforms clean and ironed and my hair neatly coiffed. They provided me the best exposure to experiences like Girl Scouts and ballet. Looking back, I can appreciate the sacrifices they made to give me a solid foundation even while working to create a better life for us all.

As my parents became more established in their careers, they started climbing the social ladder. Like *The Jeffersons,* we were "moving on up!" We relocated to the San Fernando Valley into a townhome apartment that had more than enough space for my family and my auntie, who was more like an older sister to me. The complex had a pool and a recreational room, which meant I could finally have my friends over for playdates and sleepovers. In my mind, we had made it, and I continued to thrive in every sense of the word.

When I was ten, my parents started talking about buying a home in a different city. I was overjoyed when we began looking at model homes. My soul was doing the "happy dance" as we planned to move into our very own home built from the ground up. I remember the excitement I felt prematurely deciding which room was going to be mine. I was sure it was going to be the one with the bay window and built-in bench; I could see my belongings in the room. I was not certain of the timeline of our move, but I knew this all would happen soon, hopefully before I turned eleven.

I went away for the summer to visit my grandparents in Michigan, as I did every year. I had an entire life out there full of cousins, summer excursions, and endless spoiling. It was a time to reconnect with family and give my parents a break. That year, I was especially excited to return home to keep looking for houses or find out if we picked one. The downside would be leaving my childhood friends, but I knew this was a step in the right direction. This was not my first time starting over, since I previously left my early elementary friends when we moved to the Valley. It was the necessary collateral discomfort of up-leveling. What I did not realize was that this would be the first of many times I would experience that discomfort.

Getting off the plane on my trip home, the first thing I noticed was that my mom came to the gate alone. Usually, both parents would come, but I figured my dad was waiting in the car. To my surprise, it was my auntie waiting in the car. From my younger years, I was always an empath and could easily pick up on other people's feelings. Of course, I did not realize it at the time, but it makes sense now. There was a sadness in the car. Something was not right. I could feel it. I was anxious and wondering what was wrong, and when was my mom going to tell me?

NEW REALITY
As if sensing my confusion, solemnly my mother spoke up, "Bianca things are going to be different when you get

13

home." In my mind, I started to panic. I listened through her pregnant pause. "Your father is not going to be there. He is not going to be living with us anymore."

"What do you mean?" My mind started racing about all the things my dad would do: tuck me in, take me to practice, help with homework, and help with my sister. What about the house we were buying? I went blank and cold as if the blood was drained from my very being.

Looking back, I can only imagine how hard it must have been on my twenty-eight-year-old mom to break this news to me. She was still processing it and figuring out what her new normal would look like as a single mom with a toddler and a ten-year-old. On top of that, she was on her first week at a new job. Suddenly the colorful world to which I thought I was returning was now black and white. There was a heaviness all around me—it was suffocating. I enjoyed a full decade of an unfettered childhood, truly sheltered from the woes of adult life. Now the Band-Aid was ripped off, and it was time to find my way. I was in emotional turmoil; I did not have the words for it then, but I was traumatized.

My young mind was processing and questioning, "where do I go from here?" I did not feel secure. Sure, there was food on the table, the lights were on, and my basic needs were met, but life was out of balance, and things were not right. No one answered or explained why. See, I was just old enough to be told my dad was not coming home, but no one thought I was old enough to understand why. Maybe they did not have the words for it without placing the blame or breaking down. There were many whispers in the halls, closed-door conversations, or "Bianca, go to your room and play." It was not until I met back up with my friends who lived in my apartment complex that I got the piece of information my mom had not shared: they saw my dad bringing another woman into our house. Mic drop. There you have it.

That was a major turning point in my mind. Overnight, I felt like I went from a carefree ten-year-old to a burdened tween in puberty, dealing with finding herself, and I was inwardly enraged. Just below the surface of the straight-A student were the makings of a stony heart as I became embroiled with a perverse version of the facts. I did not have the words to ask for help to process my feelings. I made up a dark version of the truth. I am not sure when I started writing poetry or journaling, but it helped pour out the toxicity that was building up inside.

Then another bomb exploded when my auntie found out her fiancé was also being unfaithful to her. More tears, more hushed conversations, more sending me to my room. In the distance, I could hear the front door opening and closing as a parade of close friends and family came in and out of the house. It was like a repass that continued for months. The house was dark, and the sounds of Anita Baker, Miki Howard, Regina Belle, Stephanie Mills, and Mary J. Blige's *Not Gon' Cry* blared as the soundtrack to our life. It is what I coined "the dark years." Hurt hearts trying to hold space for my sister and me—we were all experiencing our own version of mourning, coupled with the constant undercurrent of stress and dealing with the drama of managing my new dark reality. The first time my sister and I visited my dad was at his girlfriend's apartment—the same girlfriend my friends told me was at my house. As far as I was concerned, the two of them were the immediate cause of my pain. I wanted to scream out, "Come home, Dad! Stop this! Are we not enough? Who is going to protect us? Call more! Why did you leave me?"

As time passed, the more my questions went unanswered, the more I swallowed my pain. A buildup of unhealthy thoughts continued to skew my outlook, creating five toxic tenets based on my dark version of the truth:

1. Change means bad things happen, period, end of discussion. There is no such thing as good change.

2. My dad left me because I am not valuable.

3. Men are not trustworthy, so I hurt them before they hurt me.

4. Protecting people I care about, especially my mom and sister, is more important than acknowledging my feelings.

5. I have to be numb in order to survive.

Living by these tenets caused a string of bad relationships, a pattern of self-sabotaging behavior and imbalanced friendships. I attracted co-dependent people, feeling if I was needed, they would not leave me. After the last failed relationship, I moved back home. I was no longer a fractured child; I was a completely broken woman. I had no choice but to look inward and face myself. I did not like what I saw and definitely did not like how I felt. After some introspection, I was able to identify the beliefs that created the toxic tenets and the trauma from which the beliefs were birthed.

FACING PAIN TO MOVE PAST IT

It was not until I had the courage to go back to the moment of trauma, as the ten-year-old coming home from summer vacation to find her family dismantled, that my healing began. Going back to help the little girl inside of me has been a pivotal and necessary step to knowing who I am now and my emotional triggers.

As a life coach, minister, and spiritual healer, I need you to take away one key point. Until you go back and address the root of your emotional and psychological triggers and pain, they will repeatedly play out in your life. This is a critical step in self-awareness and growth. It will help you recognize your subconscious responses and unhealthy actions to rewrite your behavioral programs and become a better version of yourself.

ACCEPTING CHANGE

After the trauma occurred in my life, I had no idea why I was completely resistant to sudden change. Since that summer, whenever change is on the horizon, I physically and emotionally shut down. Sometimes it manifests as sickness, lack of motivation, and tears. I was aware enough to cry to release the intense frustration, but I had to consciously rewrite the program to first figure out why I associated all change as bad, then give myself the permission to go back and let little Bianca know it was okay to feel that way at the time. That feeling was valid then, but resisting change does not serve me today. Knowing the outcome of that scenario and what seemed awful at the time was for the greater good of my family. Now when that panic or trigger from sudden change rises up, the woman Bianca can let the young girl know that change is okay. It often leads to growth and up-leveling, even if it is birthed out of unpleasant situations. The main point is that it will be a continual conversation until one day you realize, "Hey, I did not have that apprehension to change. I have grown in this area." Celebrate the victory!

REASSESSING SELF-WORTH AND LEARNING SELF-TRUST

When I spiritually matured, I became aware that I had been operating from a space of low self-worth. This awakening gave me the opportunity to reassess my value. I had been unknowingly giving up my significance because in my mind, my father left me. I spent years in unhealthy relationships when I started dating—my thoughts were toxic, and I was determined to hurt and not be hurt. It was a poisonous combination of low self-esteem defined by unprocessed trauma topped with a dose of misplaced anger.

True understanding began once I realized the root of my feelings, had healing conversations with my father and other family men (as much as needed), and utilized journals to work through negative emotions and reclaim my value. I became empowered as I started to know my worth and realized that circumstances could not shape it. I read books like *Interiors* and *Value in the Valley* by Iyanla Vanzant. I connected more to my spiritual community. Thank God for a praying mother and family who stayed with me on the journey. I was doing the work to fight for my renewal, but it was messy, and I made some painful mistakes. Do not be afraid of the mess—if your intentions are to be better, you will improve. You do not get better on accident; it must be purposeful. One of my biggest breakthroughs was realizing I attracted the very untrustworthy spirits I despised because that was the energy I was emitting, and it was my expectation. The universe gave me what I asked for. The distrust I had for others did not change until I learned to manage my own decisions. In other words, I was fighting the distrust in me. I had to first value myself to make better decisions, and as I did, I built self-worth and self-trust. The two work together.

LETTING GO

Evaluating my desire to care for and protect my mom and sister has been a difficult process to navigate. At times, I have to remind young Bianca, who occasionally reappears, that it was never her responsibility to take this on— it was God's. My need to control, my constant practice of watching finances (even those that are not mine), and my desire to be the protector were all a by-product of the unprocessed emotions. Now, one by one, I deconstruct that fiction. First, by owning it, and second, by discussing with my mom and sister the guilt I have to release over not keeping my sister from everyday hurt that happens in life or not being in a position to retire my mom. This is an ongoing dialogue and spiritual work. However, I am cognizant that anyone outside of yourself has their own spiritual journey. We are all here to help each other, but the biggest thing I had to do was let go.

HEAL YOUR INNER GIRL

I am now happily married with two children; my relationship and family are evidence of my inner growth. Identifying my first experience of pain and hurt to aid in the development of the woman I am today was necessary. In addition to the steps I already shared, you can also evolve with the help of a therapist, counselor, minister, coach, or whomever you feel comfortable with on your journey. An outsider can help you see your blind spots and support your progress. Understand that the little girl inside can help benefit the woman you are today if you go back and heal her. Then you can begin to know when the present day you is operating from that space. This will be a life-changing experience, and your inner girl will thank you.

Navigating Grief and Growth

CAMILLE TELICIA, MBA

There's a saying that goes something like, "life comes at you fast and can completely change in an instant." Okay, I'm pretty sure I just made that up by combining two very different quotes, possibly from two very different periods in time, but my potentially newfound quote really sums up the story I'd like to share with you. It's funny, because even though the sentiment is one that you can understand in a logical sense, when it actually happens and you're living in and through it, it kind of takes on a new and deeper meaning. At least for me it did when my mom passed away in 2016 and I became a "parent" overnight. On that day, I knew my life would never look the same again, and in order to push forward, I had to rely on my foundation while simultaneously charting new paths.

To tell you my story, I really have to take you back a few more years to 2012. That was the year that I picked up and moved from Atlanta, Georgia to Los Angeles, California. Hollywood, California to be exact. The land where dreams are made true. I think I made that one up too. In 2012, I had just finished my MBA, and I was itching for change. I was living what I would describe as a blah, bleh, basic life. (Very descriptive. Yes, I know). I was working multiple jobs: a bar manager/bartender, a part-time testing manager in adult education, and a counselor for at-risk youth. That last job wasn't really basic. It was more so emotionally taxing, as I had not yet learned how to release the energy I was taking on from my clients, but that's another story for another book. I was also in a stagnant and slightly toxic relationship that had no future but also seemed to have no end. Needless to say, your girl needed to shake things up, and fast.

I decided I wanted to move to LA in February, visited for the first time in March, and took a one-way flight on Cinco de Mayo. The manifestation game was real, but again, a story for another book and another time. What's most important is that for three years, I was living my best single, young professional life in the City of Angels, a mere 30 minutes or less from the Pacific Ocean at any given point. I started working in the IT field and was able to move into Operations, allowing me to utilize that aforementioned new degree of mine. I was making more money than I had ever made before. I was getting healthy and into the best shape of my life. I was trying new things, making new friends, and most excitingly, I had just started my coaching business. The life reset was going pretty well, if I may say so myself, and then I got the phone call.

I remember like it was yesterday—the evening in May of 2015 when I was driving home from work and called my mom to follow up on the results of a recent endoscopy she had undergone. For the previous couple of months, she had apparently been dealing with some really bad acid reflux, and she had chalked it up to indigestion until it started really affecting her daily activities. I remember her saying to just call her back when I got home and was stationary—because that's not setting off alarm bells or anything. Sure, mom, I'll sit in 45 minutes of Los Angeles traffic during rush hour to wait for your results. NOT. I immediately pulled into a Target parking lot, and forced her to confirm my worst fear. Cancer. Stage IV. Stomach. No surgery. Chemo only. So I guess I had two life changing moments, because when she finished sharing her diagnosis, my world felt like it had turned upside down.

You see, unbeknownst to me, in the three years that I had been in LA, my mom became one of my best friends. Don't get me wrong, we never had a bad relationship, save for the typical headstrong free-spirit teenage daughter pushing back against her more traditional and old-school Jamaican mother. I remember when I left for college at 17, I secretly promised myself that I would *never* move back in with my mother again. Funnily, I actually kept that promise until the phone call. We had gotten close in my post-college years as I navigated adulthood. Then, with 3000 miles between us and only a cellphone to keep us connected, our relationship deepened in a way that honestly, I'm just now able to realize and articulate as I write this. So, when I found out that my "new" best friend had Stage IV cancer, I gave myself about two hours to be sad, and then went straight into solution mode.

Within two weeks, I had (what I thought was) temporarily moved back to Georgia, because my boss allowed me to work remotely. I sublet my apartment, I put a majority of my things into storage, I packed the rest in my car, and drove 3000 miles in two and a half days back home to Atlanta. When I arrived in Atlanta, my mom was in the hospital. Walking into that room and seeing my mom hooked up to the machines with the IVs in her arm and the oxygen tube in her nose broke me. The woman who always seemed so strong and vibrant now looked so fragile and vulnerable. This shifted something deep in my spirit. I had never been more grateful to be able to be present for someone than in that moment. I could feel her fear and see her pain in such a real and tangible way, and all I wanted to do was be as strong as possible for her and for my younger siblings. I was her emotional rock. Seriously. If she were here, she'd tell you herself. If the family had "bad" news they wanted to share with her, they'd call me and tell me first so that I could relay it to her in a way she wouldn't get too worked up about it. This is another reason why I had to come home so quickly once she gave me the cancer news. Besides the physical support, I knew that she needed the emotional support during her fight.

So it's May. I'm here in Atlanta with my mom, my sister, and my brother. Mom starts her chemo, and we're all optimistic and hopeful, because yes, it's Stage IV, but medical advancements have come so far that anything is possible. However, the truth of the matter is that even though the body is self-healing, it needs nutrients and sustenance to heal. When you have a tumor the size of a peach in your stomach, it makes it really hard to get those nutrients and to give your body the things that it needs to even begin to try to heal itself. From May to November, I was hopeful, and then around December I began to see the writing on the wall. By Valentine's Day, we knew it was only a matter of time. Three days later, she transitioned.

There's something very sacred about being with someone as they leave this earthly plain. I am forever grateful that I was able to be there, holding her, talking to her, and comforting her in her final moments. She got to transition in her home with her daughters, surrounded by love. So that brings us up to the moments that my life changed. There was the moment I lost my mother, and then the next moment when I went from grieving daughter to protective big sister and now parent to my 11-year-old brother. In that moment, I knew that it was now up to me to comfort him, care for him, and protect him from that day forward.

Can I be honest with you for a second? I have literally *never* wanted to have kids or be a parent. At all. My mom always used to dismiss my claims by saying, "Wait until you get older." Ha! Did she have a crystal ball or something? Whether it was being just a little too self-involved or not wanting to deal with the stress through which I'm certain I put my parents as a teenager, I don't know, but parenthood was not in any of the plans I had for my life. But you know what they say about your plans and God's laughter. So yes, in that moment, I became what I like to call an "alterna-mom" (Get it? I'm in the mom role, but I am the older sister by 18 years) and was left to navigate the world of parenting. The world of soccer games, orchestra concerts, doctor's appointments, discipline, preparing real meals *every* night (apparently popcorn is not considered a full meal to everyone), puberty, and grief.

Navigating your own grief while learning how to be a parent to a child who is also navigating their own and simultaneously restructuring your entire life is challenging to say the least. It's been four years, and I still can't say that I've got it quite right, but some would say that's basically the parenting experience as a whole. I am fortunate to have been given a very solid foundation from my parents that taught me self-reliance, self-sufficiency, and self-determination. I relied heavily on this foundation for the first year after my mom's passing. It was like second nature for me to shift into problem-solving, solution-finding mode and work to create this new life for my family. First, I knew that it was important to make sure that I was able to be "okay" and present for my brother. Yes, I had to prioritize my well-being. There is a reason why airplane emergency procedures tell parents to mask themselves before their children. Despite going against almost every parental instinct in the moment, the reality is that you will be unable to do anything further for your child if you yourself cannot breathe. You cannot give what you don't have. I wanted to give him stability and safety, but first I had to give it to myself.

Taking care of me looked like asking for and allowing myself to be supported. I found a life coach shortly after my mom passed who provided me the space to feel and process my grief. Remember, I not only lost my mother, but I also lost the way of life I had in LA. I was double grieving and judging my grief. She also gave me the space to work through my fears and feelings of inadequacy around being an instant parent who was suddenly responsible for a whole other human being. I ended up working with her for four years and moved on to also work through all of the other limiting beliefs and fears that came with entrepreneurship, dating, and of course, continued parenting. I also had my brother work with her so that he, too, could be supported emotionally in ways that I was unable to provide.

In addition to my coach, I invited support from our family and friends. Between the parenting advice from my father, my brother's school holidays and summer trips with his father and our aunt, the shared chauffeuring and cooking duties with my sister, and the sleepovers and rides to games from friends, the load lightened with time. Instead of trying to take on everything by myself, I shared some of the weight. In doing so, what had once felt like an overwhelming responsibility became a manageable (but still challenging) experience.

Over these last four years, alongside learning how to be supported, I've learned even more about myself. I learned how to open myself up to the lessons from every experience. I've learned how to, in addition to being self-sufficient and reliant, also be self-aware. I've learned how to be mindful of how I impact everyone around me, but most importantly the people in my care. I've learned how not to be right all the time. I've learned how to manage my anger. Okay, I'm still learning this one, but I've come a long way. I've learned what it means to really show up for someone else and how different it can look depending on what they need in each moment. I've learned just how quickly I can get from the sidelines to mid-field during a soccer game when my favorite player gets injured. I've learned patience, and I've finally learned exactly why my parents would try their hardest to be at every recital, concert, game, and track meet I had growing up. One of the most important things that I have learned and gained over these four years is unconditional empathy, especially for my parents. Choosing to see where someone did the best that they could with the resources, experiences, and beliefs available to them at that time has by far been the most profound choice I have ever made. It has freed me up to release anger, judgment, and even hurt and instead offer acceptance and love as a parent, as a sister, as a daughter, as a friend, as a lover, and especially as a transformation coach.

My life changed forever on the day my mom died, but fortunately, it did not change for the worse. Now, I by no means have it all figured out, especially on the parenting front, but what I do have is a willingness to continue to learn, grow, and expand every day. I am continuing to tap into what I feel is working best for me in each moment and following my intuition as well as my angelic and ancestral guides (Hi, Mom). I ask for support more freely, and I give a whole lot more love and good vibes to others more freely. I'm still grieving, still processing, and still navigating, but with a lot less fear and dread and a lot more peace and acceptance. While I can't say exactly if and when I'll ever return to live in LA, I've learned how to tap into the energy of that carefree, young professional, beach-adjacent woman every now and again, if only for the memory of palm trees and ocean breeze. My life changed in a moment and continues to change each day as I choose to learn something new, try something new, and release something new. I am excited about the limitless possibilities available to me because of this choice, and I am excited to continue on this journey to being the best "alterna-mom," sister, daughter, friend, lover, woman, and human that I can be. It is truly the best way that I can honor my mother's legacy.

The Perfect Life

CAROL SWANSON-CARR

Growing up in the 70s, I had a vision of my life, which was a wonderful husband, the house with the white picket fence, two children (a boy and a girl), a dog, and career. I wanted it all. The small town in the interior of British Columbia where I grew up gave me a sense of security. Everyone knew each other's families, and I could not get away with much. When I went off to college in Vancouver, it was exciting. I learned a great deal about who I was and who I wanted to be and how to spread my wings and find my independence. That independence allowed me to grow and develop into the strong woman I am. Occasionally, I look back on those simple days and realize how blessed I was.

The Canadian company for which I had been working sent me down to the States to open a chain of stores. That decision led to meet my future husband. He was an African American man born in the Mississippi Delta, and I was a white Canadian woman born in the British Columbia Rockies. I still remember my first date with him. We had been seeing and talking with each other for months, and the big day finally arrived. We were going out after I got off work. I saw him and wanted to let him know I would be ready in about 30 minutes. As I opened the door, I heard him talking with a few kids in the mall parking lot. He used a tone and texture in his voice that I had not heard from him yet. It almost sounded as though they were communicating in their own language. Coming from an all-white town in Canada, I had never heard it before. I remember him turning to me and saying "Hi, almost done?" I looked at him and said, "You're Black?" He laughed and replied, "Last time I looked I was." Of course, I knew he was Black, and I was very attracted to him. It was the way he spoke to the kids that was vastly different from the way he had spoken with me. We came from different countries, different upbringings, and diverse cultures, yet we fell in love. That first date led to more, and in four short months, we were married, and thus my journey of the perfect family began.

Now, I knew it would not be easy in an "interracial marriage." Society did not view our relationship as "proper" or "acceptable." Also, the thought of bringing bi-racial children into this world weighed heavy on our minds. My husband was working two jobs and I one when we got the news that we were having a baby. The day I went into labor with our daughter, he got the call that he was now full time. We would be moving from the Los Angeles area to the Mojave Desert part of Southern California. In my eyes, it would be a perfect place to raise children. In addition, we could survive on one income, therefore, I would be able to stay at home and raise our daughter. Life then was always changing, because 18 months after her arrival, a bouncing baby boy was born. Our beautiful son made the family complete. I almost had the perfect life, or so I thought. Looking back, I will always be grateful to my ex-husband and for making it possible for me to be home with our children. I was always trying to be the perfect wife and perfect mother. I never wanted my kids or husband to have to worry. I always wanted to be the fixer of all things and I never wanted my family to be burdened with the hiccups of life. Unfortunately, doing this led me to lose sight of who I was and my hopes and dreams. I realized I was only focusing on my husband's hopes and dreams, and I became resentful. Things also grew tense for him as he was being weighed down with the burden of providing financially for our family. This led to us growing apart, and he soon filed for divorce. The idea of divorce was a concept on which I was not raised. I was raised to stay married for better or worse, richer or poorer, until death do us part. The realization that I would be starting over at 48 was devastating.

That first year was rough. I moved in with my son and his wife as I came to terms with the shambles in which my life was in February 2013. I spent time trying to discover who I was now and what had happened to that strong-willed woman I was all those years ago. I made a trip back to Canada to see my dad in May. I wanted to share with him the news of my divorce, which would not be easy. Admitting complete failure to your father is devastating. But he looked me in the eyes and said, "Well, I was surprised it lasted this long. However, you have the most wonderful children. You need to focus on that and learn to move forward." Just four and a half months later, I would lose my rock, my beacon, and my confidant. The loss of my father that year along with a failed marriage was my rock bottom, and I needed to find my way back.

That year was tough to say the least. I did not love me anymore. The person who I had become over the years was not who I wanted to be. This next chapter of my life, I focused on finding myself and getting back on my feet financially. At times, it was hard. My actions and abilities were not in sync, it seemed. Finding a job was even harder. I was either underqualified or overqualified. I was trying my best to move forward and take the steps to creating this new life I deserved. My family had always been the most important thing to me. They still are, but I also realize the most important thing to me should be me and my well-being. I had to come to terms with the loss of my mother in my late teens and some resentment I felt towards her. Once I was able to deal with those things, life started falling into place. I moved out of my son's house one year after moving in and started to rebuild my life. I was more grounded in who I was, and as I slowly unpacked the boxes of what had been my life for so many years, I could, for the first time in a long time, see me. Being in my own home again brought such a sense of ac-complishment. I was taking baby steps back into life. Each year brought more growth and a cadence of normalcy. Fi-nally, I looked around, and I could see what I had accom-plished on my own. I had a home that was welcoming and full of love. There were still parts that needed work, but I was finally at a good place in my life.

Fast forward to Spring of 2018. I woke up one morn-ing with such a busy day ahead of me. My main priority was to get sparkling cider and donut holes for my grand-daughter. She had a father daughter dance that evening at school and would be getting her hair done at the salon. I wanted to make it special and bring treats. Before I head-ed over, I had my annual mammogram, which was no big deal. I had done mammograms for years. As I walked out to get in my car, the mail man arrived. Off to the mail-box I went, and as I opened the mailbox, I recognized the handwriting on the envelope as my own. Sitting in the mailbox were my final divorce papers. Twenty-six years of marriage, six years of trying to get the paperwork done, and 32 years of my life wrapped up and sealed in an 8 ½ x 11 envelope. A new chapter in my life was starting today.

I almost blew off my mammogram, as it was going to be the same thing: "right smash, left smash, and see you next year!" Unfortunately, this time was different, but I was not paying attention. My mind was too occupied on the divorce papers and what I needed to do for my grand-daughter that I didn't notice the hesitations of the nurse, and the fact that she kept leaving the room should have been my red flags. When she finally walked back in with the doctor, he said, "We have been trying to reach your Primary Care Physician, as we need approval from him for a biopsy and ultrasound." What was I hearing? They are supposed to say, "See you next year!" It was a blur as the nurse handed me pamphlets and the doctor said, "I have been doing this for over 30 years." I looked down at the pamphlets and heard his voice say, "You have breast cancer, and we need to get this biopsy done immediately to determine a course of action."

It was as if I was in slow motion. I walked out to my phone ringing, and my PCP was scheduling the biopsy and ultrasound. I drove off numbly and in denial of what I had just heard. I allowed myself my one pity party about this diagnosis. As I pulled up to the salon, I saw through the window my granddaughter's face. She was full of excitement. It was in that exact moment that I knew I had cancer, but cancer did not and would not have me. I was going to be around to watch her dance with her dad at her wedding. And thus, another new chapter in my book was being written. One I did not expect, but it helped me grow in so many ways.

My diagnosis came back at Stage III, triple negative breast cancer. The course of treatment would be a mastectomy and possibly chemotherapy. They would have to wait until after the surgery to make that call on chemotherapy. In August of 2018, I had my double mastectomy, and four weeks later, I went back to work. Shortly after that, I took a second job for the holidays to keep myself busy as I awaited the news on whether I needed chemotherapy. In December, I was told I would need four rounds of chemo 21 days apart. My first round was scheduled for December 14. Then on December 29, I woke up on my 55th birthday with my hair covering the pillows. It was time for it to go. I had told my grandchildren that I was sick and that surgery would help me get better. I also told them that I may need medicine that would make my hair fall out, but it was okay because it, too, was making me better. That day, we went to the movies then drove over to the salon. No one was there but my grandkids, my son, my daughter-in-law, and me. My grandkids took turns shaving my hair. Choosing to shave my hair was empowering because it was my decision. I was going to take away my hair before it left me completely. Here I come, 2019, rocking my beautiful bald head. And yes, I was told I have a beautiful bald head.

I was so ready for this chemo journey to be over with. As I was approaching my last week of treatment, I heard the words at my oncology appointment, "Your markers are not dropping, and after next week's chemo, you will start 12 weekly chemos." Wait! What? Weekly? And 12 more! I was stunned but knew it was my only option to be cured. Finally, in June, I was done with chemo and did not have to go back for four months. I scheduled my final surgery, and by September 2019, I was 18 months into this journey and four months past my last treatment, and I could finally breathe.

When I reflect on my journey with cancer, I have learned so much. I realize that had this happened years ago, I am not sure if I would have been in the right mindset to deal with it. As I grew into loving me again, it allowed me to focus on things that I had taken for granted for many years. The financial hardship after the divorce forced me to start from nothing and rebuild one day at a time. On those bad days I was battling cancer, I focused on living life one day at a time and finding joy in the simplest of things. Simply getting out of bed and making it to work was a gift. Enjoying that ice-cold glass of water was another simple luxury I would not take for granted. My original idea of the "perfect life" had changed and evolved. I found joy daily in this new journey. My advice to you is if you need to rewrite what you once hoped for, get your pen out and start writing. Allow your life to evolve, and do not burden yourself with self-doubt or think you failed. Life does not always unfold like we think it will. You are not perfect, and nobody else is, so relax. I had spent so much time trying to be perfect that I failed the most important person of all—me.

The journey to this realization has been tough at times, but no one said life was going to be easy. We will have wonderful euphoric moments, and they will always outshine our dark days. Learn to focus on today, and find that joy, no matter how big or small. Do not allow others' negativity to rob you of joy. These last few years as I have battled for my life, I realized that life is short, and you are never promised the next day. So, make each day on earth your best. Spread your joy to others. A simple hello can change someone's day. Live your life to the fullest, and remember that sadness and loneliness can be debilitating, but they will pass as you reach for your joy.

Finding My Way to Me

DANISHA JETER, RN-BSN

It's difficult to describe the relationship I had with my mother growing up. I didn't understand her until I became a mother myself. I knew that she loved me, but I often judged her by her limitations. While she wasn't much of a communicator, she was an excellent example of hard work, perseverance, resilience, and strength. However, I can count on one hand the number of direct conversations or instructions she gave me in the 40 years I had her.

As a child, I was keenly aware that I wasn't of average intellect and was quite curious. Teachers would send notes home because my inquisitive nature was often considered a disruption or a challenge to their authority. I simply wanted an explanation that made sense to me. My mom couldn't be bothered with such trivial grievances. At minimum, she worked two jobs and had no car, so she was often too tired to reprimand me. Her classic response to these complaints was a nonchalant, "Nisha, just stop." This wasn't very effective in most cases. Her indifference and arduous schedule compelled me to figure things out on my own. Consequently, I would find myself in some very compromising situations.

The subject of sex was a huge taboo. I became sexually active in middle school. My boyfriend and I got caught by his mother, and she called my mom right in front of me. When I got home, my proverbial birds and the bees talk consisted of my mother's go-to phrase for me: "Nisha, just stop." No further discussion. Well, of course, I didn't, and I ended up pregnant a short time later. I was certain she would be furious. She could barely provide for my sister and me. But when she found out from my friend's mother in whom I confided, she did not say a word. About a week later, on a school day, I was awakened early and told to get dressed. We caught the bus to an undisclosed location. There were few women outside holding up picket signs. One tried to hand me a pamphlet, but my mother quickly intercepted it and threw it to the ground and told her to get away from us. At that moment, an armed guard got between my mother and me and the protestors and hurried us inside a heavy security door. My mother filled out some papers as I gazed around the room filled with other girls and women. My name was called, and I looked to my mother. She gave me a nod to go, so I did. When I finally figured out what was taking place, an IV was in my arm, my legs were in stirrups, and I was told to count down from 100. The last number I can recall was 96. The next thing I remember, I was being vigorously shaken awake and handed some juice and then instructed to get dressed. Shortly after, I was reunited with my mother and a nurse. She asked what type of contraception I preferred? My mother answered, "She doesn't need that, she's going to stop this shit!" I was given a bag of supplies and some paperwork and was sent home. We rode the bus home in pure silence. Not one word about what just transpired. Not then or ever. This was a perfect opportunity for her to show up for me. To talk with me and give me the guidance I so desperately needed, and she blew it.

The years following, I had little supervision and way too much freedom. I was angry with the adults in my life. In my opinion, they failed me. My father resurfaced briefly during this time and confessed that he was on drugs, then disappeared again. A family dispute resulted in the sale of my grandmother's home, where we lived. We relocated to Crenshaw District, where I immediately met this handsome older guy who lived down the street. We would talk, and he'd listen to me for hours. No one before him showed me this much attention. He pursued me for a year before we officially became a couple. I finally felt cared for. I was desperate for this type of love and interest. Things quickly evolved, and a few days shy of my 17th birthday, together we revealed to my mother that I was pregnant. We had decided to have this child, and there was nothing she could do about it. I didn't care what burden it would create for her.

I had a man who loved me, and we would establish a life together. At the time, I didn't understand the commitment and responsibility I was about to take on, but it didn't matter. I resented her and was immature and naïve. At 16, with no other real example, he was everything I thought a father and partner should be. He had a job, a car, and willingness to take on his responsibility. This was my out. I could flee the emptiness I felt and finally be able to exert authority over my own life. I had felt powerless, ignored, and unloved for so long. I wanted to show my mother how much better at this I would be. I did it right. I found someone who would stick around and help me raise my child and not leave us to fend for ourselves. Quite frankly, I wouldn't be her.

My decision to become a teenage mother was challenging. However, determined to prove I was responsible, I managed to graduate with my high school class despite lacking credits from my junior year. Around school and the neighborhood, there was chatter that my son's father was involved with other girls, but he assured me it was nonsense. My attitude was, "Well, even if it is true, I am having his baby," as if it was some consolation prize. Not long after my son was born, I confirmed the rumors were true. From that point, it was a constant recurrence. He became recklessly dishonest and disrespectful. He would often be unemployed, giving him time to entertain other women. He didn't support my educational goals, saying that I only wanted to better myself to leave him. He would criticize my weight and had no problems telling me how unattractive he thought I was. In fact, one day he looked me dead in my eyes and said, "Sometimes I look at you and think I could do so much better." I was crushed but just sat there quietly trying to figure out how I got here. Yet I never considered leaving him. How I felt didn't matter. The important thing was my son had his parents together under one roof. I had something to prove and couldn't bear the embarrassment of him leaving. Plus, he was right. I had let myself go. I was working and going to school full time and didn't take the time to spruce myself up. After he said something, I tried, but to no avail.

His infidelities led to a three-month separation after a chat with a neighbor at the local grocery store. We were neighbors for several years but never said more than hello to each other. I didn't trust women back then. He had me so paranoid and threatened by their mere presence. Well, she told me that the nights that I worked, she had seen a young lady park in my space and enter my home. When I saw her enter my house with my own eyes after calling off work and parking down the street, I contemplated everything from homicide to suicide, but neither were suitable options, as both would leave my son without me. I didn't even confront them. I decided to move back with my mother the next day. Single for the first time as an adult, I jumped right into dating. I didn't give myself any time to process the relationship I just ended. This only left me more disillusioned about men. I would run into the same type of guy. They were either juggling multiple women or lying about something. It had me feeling as if I made a mistake for leaving. So, when he called right after the attack on the World Trade Center feeling vulnerable, I didn't hesitate to go back. Things were good for a minute. We resettled into our routine, and by New Year's, I was pregnant yet again.

Another child was certainly not in my plans, but reflecting on my experience with terminating my first pregnancy, I just could not relive that. When I told him, his response was that he did not want another child with me, and if I kept it, he could not promise he would stay.

Over the next few weeks, I fell into a depression facing such a decision. I couldn't fathom the thought of him leaving. I prayed and asked God to take the baby away. I did not deserve to be this child's mother. Who would even consider choosing a man over their child? I was nearly five months along before I sought prenatal care. I had resolved that I would keep my child, and if he left, so be it. Our daughter was born September 25, 2002. She was beautiful. He was present being the doting father I hoped he would be. All seemed to be good. He lost his job again shortly after she was born, so I had to return to work just six weeks after giving birth. He enthusiastically stepped up and became her primary caregiver. I began to work 60 hours per week while he tended to the kids. The next Mother's Day, I decided I needed a break, so I took a trip to Vegas. When I returned, my son, excited to see me, began to tell me about his weekend. He told me he spent the night at Derrick's house. Derrick was the son of Jennifer, the team mom of his basketball team. I thought that was odd because she was not very friendly when I met her. Then he said my daughter spent the night too. I was confused, so I asked more questions. One was where they slept. He said Derrick had bunk beds, and he slept in the top bunk. Then he said my daughter slept in the bed with his dad and Jennifer.

I did not immediately confront him this time either. Instead, I began to take a full inventory of my life and this relationship. It had been nearly eight years and two children later, and I was still suffering this humiliation and disrespect. I allowed my self-esteem and confidence to be destroyed—a clear result of allowing my worth to be attached to him wanting me. For years, I sacrificed my dignity to beg this man to love me. But in this moment, all I could do was think about my daughter. What example was I setting for her? I thought back to my mother. Although I took issue with how she handled me in certain situations, I can honestly say she never compromised herself. If something didn't serve her, she removed it from her life. She would rather be alone than succumb to such misery. My emphasis on trying to prove myself better than her was only to my detriment. When it came to this man, I was a willing participant in my agony. It was apparent that this relationship came at high cost—a price I could no longer afford. If I could not do it for myself, I had to do it for my daughter. I was terrified. I didn't know what my life would look like, but I started to plan my exit.

My intention was to have housing and childcare set up before I left, but my plans were foiled during an altercation that resulted in him putting his foot through my brand-new computer monitor. The police were called, and he was escorted out. The next year or so was excruciatingly painful. While a multitude of unexpected people and resources extended themselves to me, I found myself grieving that relationship. There were times that I considered going back just to end my emotional distress. Despite knowing full well that it was unhealthy, it was familiar and all I had known since I was 16. Life felt very overwhelming. Trying to make sense of things, I attributed my condition to my parents' shortcomings. Blaming them justified my lack of accountability. I had two children for whom to provide. I didn't need any more excuses. I needed solutions. It wasn't until I started to look at myself that I realized I had choices in all of this and chose to be a bystander in my life. I allowed my happiness to be determined by those around me. My only reprieve during this time was school. Studying was the only way to quiet the noise and keep me distracted from my heartbreak. In each vocational program I attended thus far, I graduated top of my class despite all my personal turmoil. Therefore, I immersed myself in my nursing studies. Every "A" was a confidence booster. I did so well my first year in college, I made the National Scholar Honors Society.

As time passed, I knew I needed to address my emotional damage to avoid ending up in another toxic relationship. I wouldn't be able to distract myself with school forever. I tried attending church, but it wasn't very comforting for me. Again, I am a thinker and had too many unanswered questions when it came to religion. So, I decided to seek personal development books and lectures instead. One book that resonated was Iyanla Vanzant's *One Day My Soul Just Opened Up*. She writes "Everything that happens to you is a reflection of what you believe about yourself. We cannot draw to ourselves more than what we think we are worth." I began to understand that I authored my circumstances. My perceived lack of love from my family made me somehow conclude that I didn't deserve it from anywhere. I eventually learned that love and happiness are an inside job. No one is obligated to treat you better than you treat yourself. Understanding this, I began setting some standards and boundaries. This wasn't easy at first, because I wanted people to like me. But it became apparent that in order to attract the right people in my life, I could not lower my expectations. I treat myself kinder these days and have never allowed anyone else to treat me so poorly. It was an extremely hard and painful lesson to learn, but I got two beautiful children out of the deal who inspire and motivate me daily, so I don't regret any of it. That relationship helped mold the woman, wife, and mother that I would eventually become. Through my experiences, I was able to figure out who I am, but more importantly I gained insight into who I wasn't.

The Emotional Rollercoaster with My Dad

ERIN KELLY

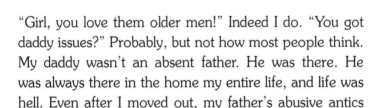

"Girl, you love them older men!" Indeed I do. "You got daddy issues?" Probably, but not how most people think. My daddy wasn't an absent father. He was there. He was always there in the home my entire life, and life was hell. Even after I moved out, my father's abusive antics continued.

It has always been said a father is a girl's first love and the example she emulates in future relationships. I was a daddy's girl, and he was my first love. I still remember all the fun and silly times growing up. As a little girl, I would put barrettes in his Jheri curl when he was asleep. I smile as I think about being woken up at 3:00 am to Curtis Mayfield blasting through the speakers and our rhythm-less selves dancing across the room. I wanted for nothing material because my dad was an excellent provider. What I did want was to hear him say I love you. Now at 39 years old, I can count on my hand how many times he said it, and it was always in response to me saying it first.

People assume because I grew up with both my parents and didn't want for anything that my life was wonderful. Just because it looked good doesn't mean it was good. Somewhere along the way, my dad made me feel inadequate. Opinions and views I had about life were ridiculed, and this planted the seed of uncertainty in me. I recall saying that I wanted to be a model and being told models were professional airheads or wanting to wear red and told whores wore red.

At around 16 years old, a shift happened, and I didn't know what version of my dad I would be coming home to. I remember being met with a slap to the face walking through the door because I had an attitude or sitting at the table eating and then looking at my food on the wall because he was mad for reasons I never knew or cared to know. I was a child, and it did not feel good to witness these events. It's like his love language was "crazy." Through it all, I loved my daddy.

My daddy was a controlling womanizer. I feared him as much as I loved him. He was a bully, but only towards women. When confronted by a man, he became a complete coward. As a kid, I saw him cause so much hurt, grief, and chaos. There were many arguments with my siblings' mothers and my mom, and some of those situations turned into domestic altercations. One Christmas, the tree went flying out the front door and onto the lawn, and each year, the tree got smaller and smaller until there wasn't one. The sad memories of Christmas became a running joke. With everything I saw, what I never got a chance to see was him being truly held accountable for any of his volatile actions.

A father never thinks anyone is good enough for his daughter, and I feel like there was always a weird competition between my daddy and the men I dated. I was 20 years old and began dating a man named Robert. He was 8 years older than me and had three children. He was wonderful to me. Life just beat us down. He was shot early on in our relationship, and his mouth was wired shut. Daddy resented him immediately, feeling as though I could have been killed if I were with him. He couldn't see how much Robert was a great man. I wanted for nothing, and he definitely treated me like a queen. I really think my dad was jealous that another man was providing for me. When Robert gave me money to buy a car, my dad was pissed. He wanted me to give the money back. His stance was that I had a father and that I didn't need a man for anything. I didn't realize then that that was him needing to control my life. I got into an accident in my new car, and the car was totaled. My heart pounded just thinking about the call I had to make. This was the last thing I wanted my father to know. My boyfriend and his daughters were in the car with me, and I knew that alone was going to send him over the edge. I was right. In a drunken rage, my dad jumped on me and pushed a dresser on me before kicking me out. I was told I could come back home in two weeks. I never went back. Two years later, my boyfriend asked my dad if he could marry me. Unbeknownst to me, the answer was no, but he asked me anyway, and I said yes. My excitement turned to disappointment, because nobody was happy for me, and most of all, my daddy wouldn't be walking me down the aisle. My relationship with Robert fizzled, and I felt my dad won.

When I was 25 years old, my parents officially split up. There were wrongdoings and infidelities on both sides and years of just being fed up came to a head. Everything seemed normal until the realization that my mom was really done caused another shift in my dad—one I never expected. He was infuriated that I did not side with him nor would I tell him where my mother was. He demolished my room in my grandmother's home, where I was living at the time, breaking everything from my makeup to perfume bottles. It didn't even matter that he was doing this in his mother's house. He didn't stop there. He stalked me, slashed tires, keyed my car, and showed up at my job where I hid under a desk, scared. I couldn't, or maybe I didn't want to, believe this was my dad. After a while, my mom arranged a date and time to pick up her stuff from the house. My dad's demeanor in her arranging the time was calm, as if he had accepted their relationship was completely done. He had not. While I was helping my mom move her things out, he attacked us. His rage exploded. As I tried to protect my mom, my dad started fighting me like I was a stranger in the street. Nothing could have prepared me to see the darkness in his eyes as he looked at me. He didn't know, or maybe didn't care, that he was fighting his little girl.

My father was arrested and bailed out of jail. Through all the years of his behavior, I knew there was more to come, but I never expected him to start acting like a crazy ex-boyfriend. Months later, I would have to testify against my dad. This was, at that time, probably the hardest thing I had ever done. So many people had opinions, and I was worried about what people thought. My grandmother disowned me and removed me from her will. My dad went to jail for a few months, and through the pain, I still missed him. After all he was my daddy. But I was still scared.

I began dating men I knew my dad wouldn't like out of rebellion. I met George, a motorcycle riding hustler, who was eight years older than me. I knew my dad would hate him, and sadly, I was delighted by all of it. He always said guys with motorcycles were the worst kind of men, but George made me feel safe against my dad. We had a good time together. He provided and did all the things I wanted to do. Sometimes I found myself unimpressed because it was rooted in me that I had a father who provided for me. At times, I think I desired for George to do more. Not because I wasn't grateful, but because I was trying to capture a feeling that I had a man who could do more for me than my dad. One day, George said to me "I'm surprised you've never been in a domestic violence relationship." He had never put his hands on me, but the statement made me wonder if he wanted to. And yes, I had been in a domestic violence relationship—with my daddy! I was so focused on feeling protected from my dad that I ran into the arms of a man who was very similar. My boyfriend was also a womanizer. When I had enough and broke it off with him, he vandalized my car. He also became a stalker, standing outside my home or following me when I was out with other people. The very thing from which I was running in my dad was in front of me with my now ex-boyfriend. Was I dating out of rebellion, or did I attract men like my dad because I missed him?

And then there was Tommy. I was getting better with the age thing. He was only 5 years older. He was different—God fearing, driven, and very passionate about life. I fell completely in love with him. He and my dad had an altercation. My dad was very disrespectful, and it almost turned physical. Tommy later said, "I'm glad nothing happened. I don't want to be the guy that beat your dad up, because that's a memory you can't take back, and he will always be your dad." He created balance for me. This man told my dad he would not always be around, and in his absence, he was to still be respectful, and neither I or he should have to worry about my physical well-being. This was the security for which I yearned, and I had it. He helped me cultivate a relationship with my daddy again. After losing my job, I struggled with depression trying to figure out my purpose and went from taking care of myself to being solely dependent on someone. Through it all, I was being loved and in love until I wasn't. Whether it was the accurate truth or different words to soften the blow of what the real issue was, Tommy told me I wasn't driven enough and that he could no longer be with me, although just a month prior he advised me to make appointments to look at wedding venues. I was now alone, unloved, and unprotected, and all the feelings of being inadequate and hopelessness rolled right back in. My daddy made me feel this same way, and yet, I wanted my daddy.

After three failed relationships, I had opened communication with my daddy. Although he had become easier to talk to, I wasn't ready to tell him everything that was going on. I had no money and was living pillar to post and needing to start over. I did, however, tell him my desire for a major career change, and he said it was amazing and was excited for me. Who was this man? This ain't my daddy! I was happy. He was listening. I learned to speak up for myself and talk to my daddy with conviction and not be ashamed of expressing my aspirations. I felt I had met a new man, because for the first time, he was not condescending. I felt heard, excited, supported, and most of all, loved.

As I was learning the new me, I was also learning about my daddy. My dad was an only child, and I attributed a lot of his tantrums and selfish behavior to this and the fact that he was raised by parents who enabled his behavior. Add in alcohol, and you have a man who loses control when he doesn't get his way. I learned my dad is battling many demons and woes of uncertainty within himself. After the passing of his parents, it came out that his mother wasn't his birth mother. None of this excused his repeated behavior, but it did help me understand him more.

My dad and I had a good drama-free run for a couple of years, and then he broke up with me again. I laugh at this because I truly feel like he is a crazy ex-boyfriend. Although I've reached out and called multiple times, he has chosen not to return any of my calls. My dad is a person who believes that the world revolves around him and that his opinion is the only one that matters. The word "toxic" is thrown around so much, but I truly feel this way about the relationship with him, and it has carried over so much into my adult life. In some instances, I was looking for validation from him. Whether he knows it or not, he was embedded in my psyche.

When you're a kid, you never imagine your life won't turn out the way you dreamed. What I've learned since becoming an adult is that people are simply people, and we want to hold them in a certain regard because of the role they play in our life. There is room for error in everyone, and I'm learning that it's okay to not have certain people in your life, no matter who they are.

I spent a lot of my young adult life searching for men who would protect me from my father. This caused me to enter into relationships with a false sense of security. I needed someone to erase all the negative things my dad had implanted in me and make me feel worthy. Although my relationships were of love, what was missing in all of them was me loving me. Feeling safe, secure, loved, valued, and worthy was my responsibility. My father's negative words about me whispered in my mind so loudly that I struggled to see my own greatness. Staying in that hurtful space was a choice, and I no longer wanted to be defined by his words. Now I get to see myself through my own lenses. I get to be in authentic relationships because I'm not looking for someone to protect me from my dad. When I released my dad's judgment of me, it gave me all the protection I needed.

I miss my dad and think of him often, but for the first time, I feel free and don't yearn for the necessity of him in my life. He will always be my dad, and I will love him through spirit from afar. The freeing of him has given me the strength to exhale. I no longer carry the indirect need of his approval. Sometimes there are triggers, and I think, "Wow, my dad doesn't talk to me." Even during times like that, I know I'd rather have no relationship than have one where I'm always walking on eggshells. True healing and restoration of relationships doesn't come with the residue of a toxic past. Maybe one day our relationship will be restored with genuine love and a mutual respect. Whichever it is, I get to choose to be at peace with it all.

The Apprehension to Love

JANISE SALONGA-WARNER

I've been told that I am a kind, loving, caring and understanding person. Hearing these compliments makes me smile and fills my heart with joy, especially coming from my four teenagers. Most parents of teenagers know that being described in this way by their kids is rare. When I was their age, I never thought that I would be described in such a way. I thought it would be the opposite. After mourning the passing of both my parents as a young girl, I became numb to those types of feelings and emotions. I felt unloved, uncared for, angry, scared, and resentful.

My mother passed when I was five years old from a heart attack and asthma attack. My father passed from leukemia when I was 10. It wasn't until after my father's funeral that I realized I had lost both of my parents. I was too young to really comprehend after my mother passed that she was gone and never coming back. Going back home after the funeral was daunting. From that day going forward, my whole adolescence was a whirlwind of emotions, therapy sessions, and feeling like too much of a burden to my family. I turned to my friends and boyfriends for comfort and made their family my "family." As time passed, some of my friends turned into enemies and boyfriends into ex-boyfriends. I often found myself lonely and afraid to open up to anyone. Hearing someone say they loved and cared about me while also being affectionate seemed like a curse, because I knew eventually, they would leave me too.

As I got a little older, I wanted to feel loved and cared for because I felt empty inside. I had so much resentment towards others, including my family. My immediate family included my sister and her husband, my stepmother, and my stepsister. My father remarried about a year before he passed. Their relationship was odd, and until this day, I believe that he only married her because he was sick. With no family close by (or at least any that we knew well), he would need someone to take care of his girls after he passed. She wasn't very motherly. We were all simply co-existing. It didn't feel like a family bond. She didn't take interest in treating me and my sister as daughters although she knew we didn't have parents. By the time I turned 11, my sister had married and moved into her own home. My one connection to my mother and father was gone. I felt more orphaned than loved. My stepmom only provided basic needs, and at that age, I needed more than that. We didn't cook meals or eat together or go on family outings or vacations. I felt like an outsider with the woman my dad left to care for me. We barely spoke to each other. There were times when we tried to really get to know each other, but it would quickly go into left field, and we'd end up not talking again. Later, this became my example of relationships and what a family structure consists of.

Bearing my children and giving birth to my own kids made me realize that I did not want them to feel the way I did or grow up feeling unloved or uncared for. Being with someone who showed me love and affection every day softened up my concrete heart. Raising kids is not an easy journey. My husband and I as parents make it our duty to always tell our kids we love and care about them. Both of us show it in different ways. My husband is the more affectionate one—he always hugs and kisses them. I am the verbal one, telling them I love and care about them always. One day I thought about why this is and realized that it is probably because of how our family showed us love growing up. When I first met my husband's family, I noticed that everyone would give each other a hug and a kiss on the cheek when greeted. This was abnormal to me and initially made me uncomfortable. I just wasn't used to it. My family didn't do that. We barely show affection or say we love one another. My sister and I expressed love by gathering together to cook and eat and gifting each other with materialistic things. Needless to say, this is another way I show my children love—by working hard to provide them with things they need and want. Everybody tells us that we spoil our children because they always get what they want. I say we just want to provide them with all the things we couldn't have growing up. Honestly, I think we've done a pretty good job in showing our kids that.

After many failed relationships and friendships, I found someone who showed me how it felt to be loved. Twenty years later, we're still together raising four wonderful kids. Now, it hasn't been a fairytale life. Believe me, we've gone through the trenches and back. We have separated and come back together. We were both young when we met, coming from broken homes, teaching each other, and growing into adulthood together. It's been a rollercoaster ride and still is, but we've guided each other through it all. I've learned that love is not only a word—it's a feeling that you can show someone through affection. As I mentioned before, this was a bad curse growing up. It took some time for me to figure out how to succumb to this newfound way of feeling. Being able to give and receive love was foreign to me, in a sense. It affected my marriage negatively with cheating, lying, and keeping secrets.

We separated for a couple years, and it was one of the hardest trials I had to endure. Although we were both involved in other relationships, it was evident that we still cared for each other. Obviously, our kids were affected by the situation, having to go from one home to another, seeing us with other people, and listening to us fuss and argue about the *right* way to co-parent. Eventually, we noticed how it affected our kids individually. Emotionally, it seemed as if they built a wall to protect themselves from getting hurt, trying to keep from showing anger and dislike. It affected their performance in school, their relationships with friends, and their lifestyles. As a result, I sunk into a state of depression. Deep down, I felt as if I failed as a wife and mother. I tried not to show it on the outside, but on the inside, I was crying for help. Thinking that it would aid in some way, I signed all of us up for therapy. I'm confident that if we had kept going to sessions, it would've made a difference on how we interacted with one another. Unfortunately, neither my kids nor my husband was receptive to it. Therefore, I discontinued my sessions as well. I've always told my kids that they can talk to me about any and everything, without judgment—that I would do my best to listen, share my knowledge and wisdom, and give advice when needed. Having this "open-door" policy is what saved my relationship with each one of them. I didn't want the wall they were starting to put up to block them from receiving love the way I blocked love growing up.

A year and a half after the separation, my husband and I began to work through the hurt and anger. We learned how to talk *to* each other instead of *at* each other. It was tough, but we realized that our kids needed us to be civil, so that they weren't influenced to pick sides and be secretive about what they were doing or saying when not in our presence. Before we knew it, we became more involved in each other's daily life once again. We had daily conversations about ways we could improve the way we communicate, how bad situations transpired, what hurt us, what made us angry, and what our relationship lacked. We believed that we could make it work this time and resolve our main issue of lack of communication. Both of us felt that we needed to be together again for all of us to be happy and hoped that it would help our kids feel whole again. And we also chose each other.

I can't speak on my husband's behalf, but I soon realized that getting back together right away was a big mistake. I was so consumed with bringing my family back together that I didn't stop to think of what I needed to do for myself. While we were separated, I should've taken the time to think about what I lacked and failed to provide and why. For instance, my husband asked me in many ways throughout our relationship to give him unconditional love. I'd say I would, but honestly, I didn't know how to provide it.

I've had many conversations with one of my best friends, and she always told me that I needed to learn how to love myself first—a foreign concept to me. It was one of her awakenings after going through her divorce and subsequent failed relationship. I saw her do the work to go from hurt to healed, and in my eyes, it was a difficult process. No one wants to be alone and feel unloved, but to keep from holding so much resentment about those failed relationships, she leaped out on faith and went through a time of self-reflection, learning to love herself through it all. She simply wanted to be loved and supported and to have someone go on the journey with her. She went through a rollercoaster of emotions. Realizing she wasn't happy from offering so much of herself only to get a little in return, she took back her life and gained so much in the end. She was able to do things she always wanted to do without a significant other judging or criticizing her and the path that God had in store for her. She took the time to listen to her inner thoughts and needs and love herself unapologetically. This provided a more genuine love with her kids. She was no longer giving her all to find someone to validate her worthiness of being loved. She became the love she needed. In the back of my mind, I had only heard people talk about loving yourself in books and in movies but not in real life. No one ever told me to love myself first so that I can give and receive love honestly and unconditionally. Growing up, it was never talked about. I had to have my own journey through discovering love. When it came to relationships, I didn't have any role models to show me right from wrong. My sister and her husband were married for years, and I saw them go through some of their own trials and tribulations and still stay together. However, neither one of them would talk to me about it or give advice on how and why they still remain together till this day. I admired their marriage simply due to its longevity.

As my children grow older and experience the ups and downs of being in their own relationships, I remind them how important it is to set and reach their own goals and aspirations and to discover their purpose in life. To learn they do not need someone else's love or companionship to feel relevant and that it's okay to be alone sometimes. To use that time to cater to their own spiritual, emotional, physical and mental needs, which are key factors to loving themselves. If they choose to share this journey with someone, both should elevate and support these areas rather than lose themselves for the sake of being in a relationship. These are things I learned late in my adulthood. I was given some of the tools to learn how to love and put myself first but became so programmed to provide for and love my kids and husband that I left myself out of the equation.

I realized that I needed to take a step back to discover and listen to my own wants and needs, especially when my mental and physical health started to decline. I attributed my current health issues—fibroids, endometriosis, severe anemia, insomnia, and tachycardia—to getting older until one day when I sat down to have a serious talk with a doctor/co-worker. We discussed a snippet of what I was currently going through in life and how I was feeling unhappy and unaccomplished about certain things and situations. She said, "Janise, you are simply too stressed!" She added that if I kept going at that rate, it could cause my health to decline even more. This was my wake-up call. From that day forward, I decided to stop working so many hours, to come home and actually relax, to ask my children to take turns doing housework, and to run errands instead of me trying to do it all. I allowed myself to be okay with lying down in my bed for a few hours to binge-watch my favorite shows. I was okay with my children cooking for me or buying me food from our favorite restaurants. I was able to start writing in my journal again and praying immensely, which to me were equivalent to going to therapy. Doing these things for myself helped calm my nerves, reduce my stress, and heal my mind, body and soul. I never realized that asking for support was a part of taking care of me. It was a part of me saying I was worthy of accepting help from others.

The apprehension to love has been an arduous journey thus far. Having that uncomfortable feeling of receiving affection has dissipated because I, too, wanted to reciprocate it. Learning how to be present with love and not just letting it be something that rolled off my tongue taught me how to feel the presence of love. Hearing my children tell stories about my love for them makes me believe that I am capable of growing that love with others, such as my future grandchildren. Seeing my children display love in our family and their relationships let me know that I have laid a foundation.

For so long, I was guarded, afraid of the love I didn't know how to give or receive, and afraid love would hurt as it did when I was a child. But love is not pain. It is spending time, showing affection, saying words of affirmation, or giving gifts. I have richly given that to my family daily. I can proudly say that I purposely give it to myself now without a bit of apprehension. That is the true love I was always seeking.

My Path to Success: The Sweet Spot

KIANA "VI" WARE

When I was 16, my grandmother was driving me to her house for the weekend, and the question arose, "What do you want to do when you graduate next year?" It was a question I had encountered plenty of times, but this would be the first person who would know my true aspiration. "I want to launch my t-shirt company." I spoke the words with confidence, knowing my established clientele, work ethic, and revenue would surely be enough to convince my grandmother I would be successful. But instead, I got her advice, "…go to school, study business, and then you will ensure your success as an entrepreneur." Well, grandma was right, but I forgot the most important part—ensuring my success as an *entrepreneur*.

My path to success thus far has been far from a straight line. As a young, brown college student from a middle-class household attending a predominately white institute, I very quickly learned there were social statuses my popularity and talents couldn't achieve. Everyone used to tell us to go to college, but no one told us how expensive that would be. As a young NROTC Scholarship Recipient graduating with a 3.98 GPA in the top 10%

of my class, I just knew that everything I had planned on my 5-Year Goals List would be accomplished. And more specifically, I just knew these goals would equal success. I had my pick of schools and scholarships, all ranging from academic to athletic to the arts, which would ensure I would never need a student loan to pursue higher education. Nine years later and $60,000 in student debt, I can honestly say continuing this marathon has been a journey of persistence.

When I went off to college I began to realize there was so much that I had neglected to learn. I was forced to exercise discipline in the form of a responsible schedule, learn budgeting, and battle with the frustrations of institutionalized racism. Luckily, I wasn't alone. My mom worked in the city, and she was always a phone call away from visiting campus when I'd tell her I needed her. For everything else, my grandmother was there. My first recipe, first flat tire, and first furniture venture, she was always the first call I'd make.

At some point, I began to realize I was in the working class of students. And I'd already made the decision that my art would be the way I paid for my wants and needs. I took on any odd job I could find and utilized all of my school resources until I found a paid internship. I threw everything I had into that opportunity. I knew every person's coffee order, and major-related or not, that's what paid for my extra expenses. I would call this part of my life **striving**.

As a student, I was broke. A 3.2 GPA and my scholarships collectively couldn't even cover my meal plan. How is that possible, you ask? Well, folks, now's the time that I explain to you what we middle-class folk call the "sweet spot." The sweet spot is when your parents make too much money for you to qualify for additional assistance, but your scholarships only cover your tuition and fees. See, what they *don't* account for is your books, technology requirements, food, gas, car expenses, or room and board. And what they *do* assume is that your parents who make "x" amount of money annually *should* be able to cover those expenses. Mine could not. I did everything a reasonable person would do—rode a bike everywhere within rideable distance, caught the train when I couldn't, applied for room and board grants, and bought the *used* books, and by sophomore year I **still** found myself homeless. I'd lost time for creating art. I was just trying to finish school at this point.

I lived out of my car that I bought with financial aid for a few months before a classmate realized it and let me move in until the Fall semester housing kicked in. Those three months between Spring and Fall semesters would fall into the sweet spot too. It's just that summers in Atlanta aren't exactly sweet when spent in a car. I would call this phase of my life **baking**. No one knew just how hard things were for me day-to-day. They only saw the happiness I portrayed with my white collar paid internship and scholarship stipend. On paper, everything was gravy, but in real life, I would've been happier to have more time painting and taking classes that actually focused on my talents. What was the purpose of paying for credits that had so little to do with running a business?

After too many hard times of working paycheck to paycheck, I decided to enlist in the Army. Surely this would break up the monotony of maintaining and cruising without a purpose. I'd call this phase of my life **rock-climbing**. Although I excelled in the Army, my time was short lived due to a medical discharge, and I found my way back home with nothing to do but finish school.

Upon my return, my grandmother was diagnosed with Stage IV pancreatic cancer and told she had six months to live. This came as a shock to us all, as she'd never smoked a day in her life. I began to lose sight of why the hell I decided to go to college in the first place. I only went because she told me it was what I needed to do to be a successful entrepreneur, yet here she was withering away before I could even graduate. I hadn't even begun to show her what I was capable of as an artist.

The next year or two is somewhat a blur of rotating shifts at chemotherapy treatments and skipping class to come wash her hair. I wouldn't trade for the world the time I spent with her instead of in class. And even after all of those stolen moments, she lost her battle to cancer. Doctors would probably call the time we got with her the sweet spot, seeing how she was still coherent and present, but managing her pain with countless medications. To see the woman who raised me wither away before my eyes was the hardest thing I ever had to endure, and my perspective on life was never the same after. Losing her put everything on hold.

We had experienced loss in our family growing up, but none that left me quite as adamant of the shortcomings in my life. For so many days and so many months, I drowned myself in my sorrows and succumbed to unhealthy habits in my daily life. I missed appointments, stopped attending classes, and drank no matter the time of day because "it was 12 o'clock somewhere." Nothing made sense anymore, and my relationships were toxic. My whole life had revolved around getting my degree, and now that the person who motivated me to do that was gone, I couldn't see the purpose in anything anymore. There were days I would wake up and ask myself, "What's the point?" I felt like I'd been missing the bigger picture my entire life, striving for the next goal and never taking time to enjoy my small winnings. I'd lost the person in whom I invested so much of my success and happiness, and because of that, I was having a hard time figuring out if my future successes were even meant to exist.

Finally, after what seemed to take a lifetime, I faced the grief process head on, and it allotted me the time to evaluate my own pursuit of happiness. I took a leap of faith and moved to a new city. I often ask myself what changed? What sparked differently in my routine of self-hate and sorrow to make me finally say enough is enough? And looking back, I think it was a series of things. In the span of a year, I'd gotten a divorce, lost my car, lost my job, and then lost three personal friends who were the same age as me. And I guess one day in therapy, it finally clicked that after all of these things, I was still here. All of those people I'd lost through the years had aspirations and ambitions and youth to give the world, yet they were no longer here to fulfill them. I remembered the proverb my grandmother used to tell me: "As long as you have breath in your body, you have purpose." So, what was my purpose? What was I truly missing that made me feel like giving up was the best alternative?

The biggest void that I found was that I had done little to nothing to nurture the core passions and values of my heart. I hadn't painted in months or written a poem in longer, and yet here I was living and breathing and wondering why no one around me seemed to know me. My passion and pleasure will always reside in the desire to create and express art. I realized that I had become so consumed with my grief and everything that would keep me busy from it that I was neglecting the things that made me me. What was I without the woman who raised me to be me? That was the question I needed to begin to answer.

My love for self-expression had always been obvious, but the development of this talent was one I kept sacred. I would do things for people, and they would say, "Wow! I didn't know you were an artist!" My heart would sink. How could anyone know me and not know that I have a love and a talent for art? You see, I believe we all fall victim to experiencing these life-changing events, the ones that shake up our routine and daily life and force us to shift gears. It is in those moments that we either shift for the better, or we keep going, foot to the pedal, no headlights on, down the same dark path as if we know where we're going. We find a sweet spot where we can accelerate and drift with no friction and stay there for a while because anything would be easier than simply turning on the headlights and seeing the madness ahead.

So, my question to you is where are you in your circle of life? Are you cruising into the sunset? Are you driving through the storm with your headlights on? Or are you aimlessly hot-tailing your way down the destructive path of the sweet spot? Once you've answered it for yourself, I want you to go a step further and ask is that serving you? Is it serving the people you love? If the answer is no, trust me, you have the tools to change it. You're the driver. Anyone else is just a passenger. Whether they're an on-looker from the side of the road just enjoying the show or in the seat next to you screaming to pull over or yelling speed up, they are still just the passenger.

For me, my greatest teacher became my grief, and this part, we'll call **reflecting**. I started with my sobriety, which fixed my tendency to oversleep and miss appointments. I started exercising again on a normal routine. I made a commitment to produce art once a week and set a daily schedule for myself to adhere to regardless of my unemployment. I wrote down all of my debts and put together a plan for tackling each bill from smallest to largest. All of these things may sound so simple, but it's the simple things that are the hardest to do when you're stuck in the sweet spot. Yes, you may know that these are the things you need to do, but are you actually *doing* them? Because up until then, I wasn't. And from the second I started and turned on those headlights, the storm got softer and slower from my view.

I was able to hone in on my vision for my design business and promote my services on my own website. I realized my ever-changing choices in careers weren't because

I couldn't make up my mind, but because I was looking for *happiness* and not money. I realized it wasn't a drinking problem I had, but that the problems I had were driving me to drink. The biggest of them all was being alone with those problems. My thoughts were always louder than the world, and that's why I had such a knack for going out in crowds of people and dancing or being around loud music. Once I put names to all of my obstacles, I began to tackle them all one by one.

It's a tough, ugly, and sometimes shameful process, but it is 100 percent worth it. I enrolled in school again and am on track to graduate in a year, my sobriety is in check, my relationships have ascended, my health is thriving, and my business is busy and booming. I have my 9-5, but I have a plan to save up and take my leap of faith after graduation. I realized after I gained control over my life that I had been running on autopilot in the sweet spot and didn't know it. The irony of the sweet spot is that it isn't really sweet. It's the oxymoron we use for uncomfortable circumstances over which we have no control and just accept. But now I can happily say that I am living a life of purpose and speaking my desires into existence.

Loss and grief come as they always do, but I'm better prepared now. Tragedy doesn't throw me off my path because it's my path, not someone else's. My grandmother may have set the foundation for my morals and values, but her legacy lives on through me. I rebranded my business after her when she passed away to remind myself why it's important to share my gift with the world. If I could tell you to take one thing away from my story it would be this:

whatever you want, go out and get it. Because at the end of your journey when your time is up, the only person who has to live with your regrets is you. When you get to that point of freedom in your journey, well folks, that is what I truly believe is the sweetest spot you can be in.

From Broken to Breakthrough

LATOYA ELLIOTT

My story began in the spring of 1974 when I was born into a middle-class Midwestern family. My father worked for one of the Big Three auto companies, and my mother had a good job with the County. They were already raising two teenage daughters when I came along. I wasn't at all planned. In fact, I was supposed to be impossible since my mom was told she couldn't have more children. God had a different plan. My mother always referred to me as her "change of life" baby. My dad admitted he secretly hoped for a boy, but he was quick to say he was happy with his three girls. My sisters had very different reactions to my arrival. Gina—13 years my senior—was cool with it. My big sister didn't share her enthusiasm. Valerie was 15 years old when I was born and very embarrassed that our parents were having a new baby. She often said her friends couldn't wait for me to arrive; but she was dreading it and thought our parents were way too old to be having another child. She always told that story to me with her nose a little frowned up and pointed in the air as she shook her head in disbelief. Each time she told it, she ended by saying how much of a blessing I was to our family even though she didn't want me at first. I smile about that memory now. It was one of many times throughout my life that Val would call me a blessing or tell me how proud she was of me.

My sisters were special and always my biggest supporters second only to my parents. And though there was a large age gap between us, we were close. My relationship with them was my safe place. They were two people in my world whom I knew would be in my corner no matter what.

Growing up in a tight-knit family has its perks. I never lacked love, support, or encouragement. Thinking back, my family was like body armor for me. The protection I needed to keep me unscathed from outside influences. But tight families can be a blessing and a curse. A blessing because they love hard, create traditions, and make lots of memories. A curse only because any damage to it can be destructive to your soul. In 2003, I experienced the first chip in my armor when my father died. I'd suffer loss before, but never at that magnitude. His death drastically changed my family dynamic and me in the process. Daddy had been sick for years. But his death was still unexpected. It rocked me to my core. It was a level of grief none of us had experienced. I held my sadness close, not even sharing it with Val and Gina. I didn't talk about it much, and certainly not with them or my mom. Why not? In my mind, they had enough to deal with. They didn't do or say anything to make me feel that way. It was my coping mechanism. I was a strong Christian woman who knew the power of prayer and the Word. Talking about how sad and messed up I am wouldn't solve the problem. So, "Put your big girl panties on, Toya. Pray. Read your

Bible, and go on." That's what I told myself even as I was struggling, filling my days with busyness but never dealing with my grief. You can't change what you won't face. I know that now. I went to a grief counselor one time after a friend suggested it. But just that once. I was more concerned what folks might think because, you know, "Black people don't go to therapy," especially Christian Black people. So on top of grief, I added shame to the mix. What a great combination!

Years went by, and we adjusted to our "new normal." Our family now included four grandchildren. So traditions that my parents started with my sisters and me continued with them. We experienced highs and lows, celebrations and sadness. Life moved on, and it seemed good. Two years ago, it all changed. 2018 proved to be a rough year from day one. It was nothing but misery and struggle. One family member after another fell victim to either illness or death. I couldn't catch my breath. And just a few days after Thanksgiving, Val died. Talk about a shock to my entire world! I was turned totally upside down and felt like I was locked in a nightmare. The earlier part of that year, she battled illness, which wasn't new because Val had been plagued with sickness for years. But she had come through an extraordinary fight—the brink of death. She'd gone through so much and rehabbed her way with prayer and family support back to us. We'd just celebrated a wonderful Thanksgiving at my house. She was all smiles, and there was plenty of laughter. We had so much to be thankful for, and we enjoyed the family time together. How could it be just a few days later, and she was gone? After all she'd gone through and all the prayers of healing that brought her back, she still died. I just could not reconcile why and what happened in my own mind. Why?!

In the weeks after Val's death, I was spiraling. My grief took me to a new low. I was in the Valley of Nothing Matters. I didn't care about anything and I was just existing. I'd often get little to no rest, falling asleep in the comfy chair in my family room every night. I found it hard to pray or read scriptures. I was up to the wee hours of the morning because my mind would be racing with thoughts that wouldn't let me sleep. I didn't have the energy or even desire to keep up with normal family responsibilities. I was doing the bare minimum to take care of my husband and kids. I wasn't as engaged in their school work. Before my sister's death, my family was the center of my world. I ran my household like any good manager. I knew everyone's schedules and maneuvered the logistics of our lives with skill. However, grief turned me into a shell of myself. I was failing in those roles, and I knew it. I couldn't seem to pick myself up and move on this time. I was caught up in depression, and I didn't have the strength nor the will to pull myself out. The crazy thing is no one knew. Like always, I went on with the routine of life. I continued to show up where I was expected even if I was disconnected. I needed to deal with myself and my grief.

So, how did I get on the road to healing? First of all, my circle of family, friends, and church set me in the right direction. Proverbs 18:21 (AMP) says, "Death and life are in the power of the tongue..." When you are in a low place and your faith is faltering, you need someone to speak life into your situation. I remember two encounters that gave me some perspective. One day, an Elder at my church told me about his dream. In the dream, he saw a lot of his relatives who had passed on getting into a car. They seemed to be preparing for a trip, and he kept trying to get in the car too. They told him he couldn't go with them. He looked at me and said, "Do you know why I couldn't go?" At that moment, I couldn't connect the dots. I'm sure I gave him a blank look. He said that he wasn't allowed to go because he wasn't finished with his assignment. He gave me that look a person gives when they want you to grasp the lesson they are trying to teach. He continued on telling me my sister's assignment on earth was done. But I still had work to do. I didn't want to hear that. When you're hurting deeply, you don't see or hear clearly. Honestly, I was a little resentful about people trying to pull me out of my hurt. Looking back, I know that their pushing and prodding was designed to keep me from drowning in my own self-pity. They could see I was dying spiritually, and they were throwing me a lifeline.

On another occasion, I had a conversation with my pastor. I shared with him how I didn't care about anything. Nothing mattered to me. At that point, I think I was ready to throw everything away. When I say throw everything away, I don't mean end my physical life, but I had no desire to really live. I wasn't interested in taking an active role in my life. I was just existing, and that was okay with me. Nobody knew how broken my heart was. Sickness took my father from us, and now it had taken my sister too. My sisters and I were a unit. Our unit had been cracked, and the crack could never be fixed. It was permanent, and I was devastated. My pastor listened to me pour out my feelings. I hadn't really been able to do that with many people. My family was hurting just like I was. Following my same MO, I didn't want to saddle them with my pain. Pastor gave me lots of good encouragement that night. But out of all the things he said, I remember these two words the most: "Don't stop." That night, he told me don't stop. At the time, I related his words to ministry. Don't stop singing. Don't stop preaching. Don't stop teaching. Don't stop participating in ministry. However, as I journeyed through my healing process, those two words encouraged me. I often heard him say "don't stop" when I wanted to give up. The words became my motivation. I can't stop. I must keep going. I'm not done. God still has work for me to do. My assignment has not been completed.

I knew I couldn't get whole on my own and decided to try grief counseling again. This time, I faithfully saw my therapist. She helped me work through my feelings, which were a jumbled mess. She gave me strategies to navigate the journey of grief and taught me how to give myself grace if I suffered a setback. I learned how to share the load with those who loved me so I wasn't traveling alone. Most importantly, my sessions revealed that I had not dealt with unresolved feelings about my father's death. I was still carrying around that loss and anguish, and my sister's death compounded my situation. Instead of dealing with my brokenness after Daddy's death, I swept up the pieces and put them away in a box. I never fully faced it or allowed time for my healing. If I was going to be better, I had to tackle that old hurt too. I was carrying around years of pain. The process was not pleasant, but it was necessary for my healing. It's not enough to cry and let it out. Talking through each emotion gave me an understanding of where I was and a new strength to face my truth. Facing each emotion head on set me free. Putting words to emotions is healing.

No healing for me could truly come without God. He is the Master Healer. I needed to connect with Him if I was going to be completely whole. Connecting with him didn't mean going to church or doing the work of ministry. Connection comes through relationship. And my relationship with God had suffered. I needed to get back to communing with Jesus. Don't get it twisted, He never left me. Even when I felt disconnected, I still knew He was there. I knew He was working on my behalf, and I could feel the prayers of others working too. I needed to return to the place of intimacy with my God. Prayer and meditation in the Word brought about restoration. Some days, my prayer time just consisted of lying quietly on my bed listening to instrumental worship music and focusing on one or two of my favorite verses. I found this to be a great way to stop my mind from racing, uncluttering it, and making room for me to connect with Him. These moments with God gave me the greatest peace. Even on rough days, praise and prayer would pull me up. The old saints said that a song and a little talk with Jesus makes everything alright. I found that to be the truth for me. My relationship with Christ has always been my foundation. I just needed to get back to that place.

The night before my sister's funeral, I had a long talk with my cousin about Val. We talked about what she meant to both of us and the impact her death had on others. The end of her life was felt deeply by so many people. We recounted story after story that we'd heard in the days since her death and concluded that Val left an indelible mark on every person with whom she came in contact. We called it legacy. Val had left a legacy more valuable than money or possessions. The next day at the funeral, I saw how big of a difference she'd made. Every speaker shared how Val made their life better and brighter. Her life made a difference in the best way because she made a difference in the lives of others. From that moment, I knew that all my gifts, talents, and witty ideas must be used up before I leave this earth. Sure, I knew that before, but the loss of my sister catapulted me into a greater sense of purpose.

Since her death, I have felt this urgency. An urgency to get things done. An urgency to answer the call on my life. An urgency to not waste any more time. Loss changed me. I don't really remember what I was like before my father died, and Val's death changed me even more. Though grief and loss are treacherous, the woman I am now is stronger. The woman I am today has unshakeable faith. I've walked through grief, reached that place called acceptance, and come out on the other side healed. I know it sounds cliché, but I found purpose in my pain. Do I still cry in the shower sometimes? Yes. Have I stopped missing her? Absolutely not. Do I feel the weight of her absence immensely? Of course. But every day, I wake up driven by my choice to live on purpose and in my purpose. And if I want to follow in Val's footsteps, I can't waste time. My legacy is on the line.

How Breast Cancer Changed My Life

LAWANA HALL-CONKLIN

Yes, you read that right. Before I was diagnosed with breast cancer, I really wasn't living my best life. I was overweight, I was depressed from a failed marriage, I had high cholesterol, and my eating habits were not that great. Burying both my parents and suddenly becoming a single mother of three sons had taken its toll on me, and I just stopped paying attention to my self-care needs. I never imagined what life would be like after my parents passed away, nor did I get married with the intention of getting divorced, but there I was, living in unfamiliar territory.

Food became my comfort, and the pounds were packing on. I did go to the gym three to four days a week, but that was really just to socialize and post my location on social media. I needed to get serious about my health, as I was not getting any younger, and the path I was on would have led to many other weight-related health issues. I wanted to be healthier, more productive, and physically fit, but I just wasn't motivated. One night, during my nightly prayer, I asked God to give me the willpower to not just make better life choices but take control of my health. I surrendered myself to God in that prayer.

So, I bet you are wondering how all this relates to how breast cancer changed my life. Allow me to explain. That night when I prayed, God answered my prayer. He took something so scary and turned it into the most amazing experience. This is the story of how breast cancer changed my life.

THE DIAGNOSIS

I was honored when my dear friend and online pastor contacted me and asked if I wouldn't mind speaking to his online class at "Discover You Academy." You see, I had participated in the same online class in 2017 when it was just a pilot program. This program is designed to help you discover your blueprint, realize your potential, and find your place. The program was instrumental in growing me personally and professionally. As you can imagine, I was thrilled to share my experience with his 2018 class.

The date was set: January 29, 2018. The session was awesome, class participation was great, and his students were engaged. At the end of the session, I remember saying to his class, "I continue to set my goals without fear. Obstacles are like ridges and rocks on a mountain. You need those obstacles along your path to help elevate you to the next level." At the time I said those words, I had no idea that a major obstacle was about to cross my path.

February 26, a little over three weeks after speaking at "Discover You Academy," I had a women's wellness exam. It was quickly followed up by an ultrasound of my left breast, a biopsy, and then an MRI. My fear would be faced, and my faith would be challenged.

Needless to say, when I heard the words "Lawana, you have breast cancer" my world was turned upside down. Everything instinctively became surreal. My first thought was, "You got the wrong person! This isn't supposed to happen to me, God wouldn't allow this to happen to me. I pray, I pay my tithes, I go to church. No, not me."

The doctor informed me of my test results and what my possible next options would be, but I couldn't comprehend the words that were being spoken. It was as if I drifted off to another place where nothing was real. For a brief moment, time had stopped, and I was existing outside of my cancer-inflicted body, looking at myself like a reflection in the mirror.

As the tears ran down my cheeks, I instantly thought of my deceased parents. Wondering if my mom was disappointed in me for allowing this to happen to me. I needed my dad, wanting to close my eyes and bury my head into his chest and hide in his protective arms. I began thinking back, trying to recollect any guidance they may have given me along the way to deal with something like this. They both prepared me for so much, but nothing prepared me for this. My play sister Mello sat beside me speechless. Tears were streaming down her face too. This was real. My new reality, my biggest fear had come to fruition. I had breast cancer.

The nurse handed me a file containing my results, several doctor appointments, and a stack of literature on cancer associations and support groups. She could tell that I was overwhelmed by the news I had just received. She touched my hand, looked me in my eyes, and said, "I am a breast cancer survivor. It's been 10 years for me. I am doing fine, and so will you. It's true that if you choose to fight this cancer, you will lose your hair, but it will grow back. Your breast may be altered, but you are a beautiful woman, and whatever direction you choose to take, you will remain beautiful. Think of the journey you are about to take as a second chance at life. When you are done with cancer treatments, brand new cells will have generated throughout your body. New hair, new fingernails, even the blood that will run through your veins will be new. You will be made brand new. Early detection is vital, and you are fortunate that we found it when we did. Your cancer is treatable. You are blessed."

PREPARING TO FIGHT

I took a day to let the diagnoses just settle in. It felt like a really bad nightmare. I prayed, "God, my sons and I have recently lost so much. Lord, please don't let my kids lose me too." I was so afraid. I held on to the words of the nurse who was a cancer survivor: "You will be made brand new." I wasn't sure what I was about to face, but I knew that this would truly be the fight of my life. *For* my life.

I made several attempts to read through the literature that was given to me, but my brain would not allow me to comprehend what I was reading. Every woman on every brochure looked sick. They looked old and frail, with funny looking wigs or wearing ugly head wraps, no eyebrows and no make-up. If cancer had a face, it would look like how these ladies did. Even when I searched on the internet, every video was more of the same. More hideous head wraps and housecoats hanging off under-nourished women surrounded by family and friends, all with facial expression of sorrow and defeat. Was this to be my fate? Would cancer treatments have me looking like "cancer"?

Well, I refused to look like any of those women. I was a Black woman in my 40s, but I was often told that I look like I am in my 30s. I dressed like I just came off the cover of *Forbes Magazine*. My hair extensions were always on fleek, and my high heel game was fierce. I was a Senior Business Administrator/Trainer for a manufacturing consulting firm, a successful and talented cake artist, and a proud single mother of three intelligent and handsome sons. My priorities had been my 9-5 career, my cake business, and creating a good life for me and my kids. I worked hard for me and my family to live comfortably, and we were finally adjusting to our new normal. Being diagnosed with cancer could change everything.

It was at that moment I remembered what I had told my friend's class. I didn't know how this journey was going to end, but I knew that God wouldn't allow this obstacle to come and defeat me because he would carry me over it. God had seen me through some difficult times in my life, and I knew he would see me through this too. As much as I wanted to give up and surrender to my fears, I refused to make excuses. I refused to waste any time feeling sorry for myself or succumbing to the stereotypical images of cancer and cancer treatments. Now was the time for me to focus on the battle ahead of me and get ready for the fight of my life. I remembered the night that I surrendered to God. I knew then that God was going to use me. This "test" would be my "test"imony.

Over the next few weeks, life was hectic. Appointment after appointment. I felt like a research rat. "I had been stuck with more needles, had more X-rays, test scans and procedures performed than most people will have in a life time." (I stole that quote off of a T-shirt, but it's true.) With Mello by my side, I made every appointment and went through every procedure without any setbacks or issues. Then the day finally came—my first day of chemotherapy.

CHEMOTHERAPY

There are several medical definitions of chemotherapy. Here is my definition: "Chemotherapy is a combination of poisons injected in your veins designed to kill every radical cell in your body, good and bad. As your body fights to recover from the loss of these cells and begin to heal, you get injected with more poison all over again."

On our way to the cancer care center, Mello and I talked about anything and everything that came to mind, except for the obvious. Even though we had both done tons of research, there still was a sense of uncertainty. At this point, there was no turning back. The port had been surgically placed in my chest, so the medications would go directly into my jugular vein. I was prescribed several different allergy and nausea medications and instructed to take them before arriving at the center that morning. All the research in the world could not prepare me for what

I was about to encounter. Like a boxer prepares to fight his opponent in the ring, all the doctor appointments, exams, and procedures had prepared me for this moment—my fight with cancer.

My heart dropped when the nurse appeared in the doorway of the treatment room and called my name. I got on the scale: 252 pounds. I had no idea I had gained so much weight. The nurse went on to explain that I would have to weigh in every time I received treatment so they could adjust the medications accordingly. I sat down in a recliner next to the window that had a beautiful view of the Pacific Ocean. Mello began to record with her smartphone as the staff at the cancer care facility did their best to ease my mind about the procedure. I won't lie, I was scared.

I reclined the chair back and fluffed out the blanket across my legs that my best friend's mother knitted for me. Looking around the room, one patient was sleeping, another on her smartphone, and one woman was just gazing aimlessly out the window. The room was quiet and depressing.

The staff confirmed my schedule. They explained that it would take a total of six hours to push all the medicine through. Every three weeks, I would receive chemotherapy for a total of six treatments. The first nurse came and cleaned my port, sprayed this extremely cold solution over it, then inserted the needle, starting an IV saline drip. A few minutes later, another nurse appeared wearing what looked like a hazard suit holding a medicine bag. She confirmed my information on the bag then she attached the bag to my IV. Round 1, the bell has rung. Let the fight begin.

Let me just say, fighting cancer is not for the faint at heart. With all the research I had done, I was still sucker-punched by the side effects of treatments. Medical menopause, neuropathy, edema, and cognitive dysfunction (more commonly known as chemo brain). Those terms, along with a few others, had become part of my daily struggle. There were times that I wanted to quit and give into the stereotypes that I saw on the pages of those cancer brochures. Fear and exhaustion were consuming me.

During my fourth chemotherapy treatment, I was scrolling through YouTube on my smartphone looking for an inspirational message. I came across a sermon titled "Faith that Conquers Fear" based on Isaiah 41:10 (NIV): "Fear not, for I am with you; Be not dismayed, for I am your God. I will strengthen you, Yes, I will help you, I will uphold you with My righteous right hand."

The pastor preached about how fear is destructive and can have a progressive effect, that God did not give us the spirit of fear. He said to have Faith in God and believe on His promises. Faith that conquers Fear.

Normally after chemotherapy, I would go and get some sort of savory, rich and decadent comfort food. Comfort food was safe and familiar to me. This practice would give me temporary satisfaction, but it was not helping my weight issue. I gave myself permission to eat until I was stuffed, hiding my fears in food, then would feel guilty and depressed afterwards.

That day, I decided to do something different. I started to research foods that are good to consume while receiving chemotherapy. No longer giving into my fears, I committed to changing my eating habits. I began to eat for the nourishment of my body. It didn't matter if it tasted good to me. I was giving my body what it needed to help fight cancer. Day by day, I felt myself getting emotionally stronger and feeling better. My energy level began to improve, my complexion cleared up, and I started losing weight. On the days that I struggled with my food choices, I would reference Isaiah 41:10, and my willpower would be renewed.

I won my battle against breast cancer, and I am winning the battle of the bulge. The scars that cancer left me with are my beauty marks and a reminder of God's promise and that His grace is sufficient. I am stronger, wiser, and much healthier than I have been in my life. I went from a size 18/20 down to a size 12/14 and still progressing. Diet and exercise are now a part of my daily routine. I continue to research how what we put in our bodies affects our health, sharing my testimony with other women in similar situations.

It's crazy, but I am truly grateful for my journey. Breast cancer is what motivated me to drop the excuses and start living my best life.

From My Point of View

MINA LONDON

I will never forget the reaction of my mother when I reminded her about her brother whooping my ass back when I was a kid. She let out a giggle that shocked me. I always wondered if it was a nervous laugh. Was it funny? Or maybe it was the way I said it. No one knows the pain I dealt with in the company of my schizophrenic, drug-addicted uncle. He was a bully who was in and out of jail, and as a child, I thought he was scary. No one ever asked me what I felt about him. Terrible memories of him are stuck in my head. That trauma will be with me for the rest of my life. It takes an enormous amount of strength and energy to act as though nothing happened and to keep functioning while carrying those unforgettable memories as a young child. Family members should be held accountable for their actions, no matter who they are. Oftentimes, those actions are swept under the rug, and the victim is left to bury the hurt and silence the pain while the offender continues on with no consequences, free to do the same actions again. People should recognize how powerful and vital their influences are to a young child. Our environments influence our behaviors, moods, and interpretations of the world. According to the National Survey of Children's Health (NSCH), nearly 35 million

U.S. children have experienced one or more types of childhood trauma. It's so important that children be protected at all costs, even if from their own family. I hope this generation and the ones after are aware of how their childhood affected them. May their awareness help put their energy into healing.

Growing up with drug addicts, alcoholics, and in-and-out-of-jail family members was all normal to me. My cousins and I saw unbefitting things for a child, such as a crack pipe in the backyard while playing. We would be restricted from playing outside for weeks because my uncle would be out there on a rant with his disorderly speech, breaking things, taking showers with the water hose, or asleep with his sleeping bag and pillow. It was best to stay out of his way whenever he got like that because he would take his frustrations out on you if you got caught in his crossfires. I always heard that no family is "perfect," so I thought my situation was like everyone else's. Oh, was I wrong! Taught at a young age that you don't tell family business and that whatever happens in the house stays in the house, I silenced my voice to ask for protection. I knew if I told anyone what I was going through at home, nothing good was going to come out of it. I knew it would make things harder on us. I heard countless horror stories of kids being put in the system or being sexually abused or starved, never to see their family again. That frightened me extremely. Just thinking about being one of those kids made it not worth talking about because no matter what he did, he was always welcomed back, and it wasn't worth risking being away from my mom and sisters.

Now that I am a mother, I understand the sacrifices we make daily so our children can have everything we didn't have. In no way will I discredit my mother's and grandmother's love for me, because they showed it often, but love was just not enough. I needed love to include protection. I always felt my mother spoiled me because my biological father wasn't around. Even when she probably wanted to say no, she still gave me everything I ever wanted, and for that, I am grateful. I was a sensitive child. I had things rather than attention, and that was no perfect remedy for a child like me. We all have parents. Did they do everything right and meet the needs of every child? No. Everyone just did the best they could with what they had in the world around them. My mother worked nine to five, five days a week, which left me with my grandmother and her dysfunctional son, my unstable uncle.

One incident I remember is when he was talking to me and I started to walk away while mumbling smart remarks under my breath. He rushed behind me, throwing me to the ground with his hand around my neck, hitting my head on the floor and him yelling how disrespectful I was. His face showed this raging anger, almost like he was a different person. As he continued yelling many other words, none of which meant anything to me, I just wanted him to let me go. I wanted to run to my grandmother and cry about what he did *again*. I cried so hard that I couldn't breathe, not because his hand was around my neck but because the shock of it all literally took my breath away. I was only nine years old at the time. I knew my mother's work phone number like the back of my hand, but I thought she would get in trouble at work due to the number of times I would call. Honestly, I just wanted her to rush home so she could scream, yell, and let him know how unacceptable that was. I needed that sense of protection from her, and I never received what I was longing for. That made me feel not worthy to fight for. I felt ignored and not good enough.

My grandmother would always kick him out the house but always allowed him to come back. I would wake up in the morning, and he would be back like nothing ever happened. I would look over at my grandmother and give her this disappointing look followed by "Momma!" That's what I liked to call her. She called that behavior unconditional love for her children. I called it weakness. Before going to bed at night, I would double check the doors and windows to make sure they were locked so he couldn't get in the house. I would have this recurring nightmare of him breaking into our home time and time again because he wanted to be back. In this dream, I had a whole escape plan if anything were to ever get out of hand. I told myself I would really put that escape plan into action if I ever needed to. I had the same dream until I eventually moved out at 19 years old.

In many ways, violence showed up and played a big role in my life and how I interpreted the world during my childhood. In the third grade, I had a crush on a boy in my class. He would act as though he liked me when nobody was around, but the moment he got around his friends, he would hurt me. Once, he pushed me into a brick wall. Another time, he firmly grabbed my arm to get my attention.

Maybe he was showing out for his friends, or maybe he was dealing with his own problems at home, but why did I allow this to happen? Why did I think this behavior was normal?

I normalized this behavior because it was simply normalized at home. I assumed my mother wasn't going to stop it and that I should just try to cope. I switched schools later that year, which was a blessing in disguise. I never told anyone about the incident with my crush until now, and I held guilt for allowing it to happen. The older I got, the more fighting became fun. I always felt I had to prove to myself that I wouldn't allow anyone to mistreat me anymore. I would practice "play fighting" with my cousins to get better, but then the fights always turned into real full-blown fights. I had fights at school a few times and never really understood why my behavior went from quiet shy girl to please try me. That attitude remained alive in me until I matured and analyzed why I was so mad. My environment affected my mood. I would feel sad, angry, alone, helpless, and emotionally neglected. I didn't know how to process some of the things that happened to me because they were never talked about. I didn't have a safe space to express myself. Holding in my feelings took me to a dark place where I blamed everyone for my mood and actions. I didn't feel like anyone cared enough to understand me and see everything I was battling. Violence and neglect in my life left traces on my mind and emotions.

From my adolescent years through my early twenties, I wasn't committed to healing and navigated through life avoiding the feeling of discomfort. I thought that masking the pain and shutting down anything that disrupted my peace would make the discomfort disappear. Instead of facing my problems, I avoided the subject entirely. In all honesty, I didn't have the knowledge or tools to heal. How would I begin to explain to anyone how my child-hood truly affected me? I got good at putting a Band-Aid over unresolved problems only to realize they would rise again later. In today's world, we are taught only the strong will survive, and strong people don't complain, we just deal. I am here to tell you that is far from the truth. Ex-pressing your feelings and emotions does *not* make you weak. Holding in your suffering will only bring more pain. Healing from any feelings around trauma is not easily done. No matter the experience, it was part of the jour-ney helping to shape me, but it does not define me. Who I am today is not who I was years ago because I no longer wanted to focus on what happened, I'd rather focus on a solution. Where focus goes, energy grows. I began to shift my focus to healing and creating peace, forgiveness, and authentic happiness. I was determined to break the generational cycle of silence before it repeated with my children. I am learning from it, I am growing from it, and I'm letting it all go.

The biggest turning point for me to begin my heal-ing journey was when I became a wife and mother of two beautiful beings. My little family is teaching me true selflessness and unconditional love. I didn't want to love from a place of hurt and continue the cycle with an un-healed heart. They became my "why." Why I get to be mentally healthy and why I chose a path of healing. Most importantly, my why makes me strive to be the best version of myself, to always put my best self forward. May my children never have a childhood from which they have to heal. I want to be everything for my family that I didn't have growing up. I get to lead by example and show I will always be available to listen and guide them and make sure they feel safe, protected, and always free to express themselves. I am proud I married someone who wants to instill the same values into our children. It's important that our kids see a healthy and loving relationship built on a foundation of trust, honesty, and communication encapsulated by God's grace. So many of us had to learn on our own what a family really looks like. I choose to demonstrate that every day for my babies.

I was blessed to discover my love for writing at a pretty young age. Writing became my outlet for bottled up emotions, and that helped me express myself so boldly and honestly. I didn't have to be ashamed or silence my truth. This helped me build my confidence and empowered me to have a voice. My writing is an expression of me on paper, a vehicle to feel whatever emotion I need to release. Dwelling in my past was only preventing me from moving forward in growing, evolving, and enjoying life. Writing gave me a sense of emotional nourishment by helping me see my potential. My journey has prepared me to this very moment.

God has made his presence known in my life with divine intervention. He continues to lead and guide me in the direction I should go. I'm grateful for every lesson that tried to destroy me. It only rebuilt an even stronger version of myself. Knowing that there is a plan for your life gives you the resilience to get through any situation. Doing what you love and surrounding yourself with whatever makes you happy helps you see your value, reminds you to not settle for anything less than joy, love, and peace. You owe it to yourself to live a life with intention. Embrace who you are—your dreams, your story, your imperfections. You're worthy of love, happiness, respect, and all that is required to feel safe and protected. Healing is a journey. Wherever you are in your journey, love yourself and be patient with yourself as you're learning. Be gentle with yourself because there are many layers to you. Do the work to improve one day at a time. Dig deep to listen, honor and surrender to what it is that your inner child needs, and pour that love and energy into yourself. Honoring your inner voice is the beginning of feeling liberated. Your journey will not be perfect, but it will be worth it. Do not let your unspoken stories eat at you. Even if no one understands you or no one seems to care, you still matter. At the end of the day, show up for yourself because no one will love you like you love you. It's our job to lead our own life. We are the only ones responsible for our own healing. So here's to living in your authenticity and to speaking more about the hard stuff that no one ever wants to talk about. Celebrate your healing and willingness to change your life. Cheers to raising children who don't have to heal from their childhood. Most importantly, celebrate you because you are and will always be enough. I love you, Shenomenal Woman.

Losing Izaiah

MKA MORRIS

I will never forget the day my life dramatically changed. It changed in a way that I never imagined it would or even could. The day was Friday, and the date was May 13, 2005. Up until that day, I was living and loving life to the fullest with my two incredible heartbeats—my children. My oldest was my eleven-year-old daughter, and the youngest, my son, Izaiah, who was two. These two kids were the air I breathed. Life had purpose because of them. Our morning started pretty mundane. It was a bright, sunny, typical spring morning. The night before, I slept in Izaiah's bedroom. I was awakened by him and his sister playing. They were early birds. I looked at my phone and realized that we were running late for a planned family road trip. I got up, kissed my baby boy, played with him a little, and went into my daughter's room, and found her excited to be home and ready to take off for our trip to South Carolina. I went to the kitchen and made some salmon cakes, one of Izaiah's favorites. My daughter helped herself to a bowl of cereal. She was pretty self-sufficient. I decided to take my shower and get the kids ready for our weekend getaway. While in the shower, my son would run in the bathroom and pull the curtain back. I would splash him with the water on his face, and he would run away giggling, so excited by our game of peek-a-boo with a twist. I loved our mornings that weren't filled with traffic and rushing to prepare for work and school. So I took my precious time and enjoyed every moment of it.

I finished showering and decided I'd get dressed in my living room since my bedroom was on the far end of the apartment. I had to listen out for the toddler, who, by then, had run between the living room and his sister's room. I had the most random thought on this day that, "Wow, he's now two years old and probably shouldn't keep seeing me naked." I asked him to go to his room and put his book away as a distraction so I could get dressed alone. He ran into his room. I knew I had about a cool minute before he would reappear to finish playing with me. I dried off quickly and almost had my jeans pulled up when I heard the blinds hitting my son's wall. I knew he needed my attention quick, because he had been told not to play in the windows in the apartment. They all were floor to ceiling. As I entered his room, I glanced at the window. No sign of him. I walked quickly to the closet thinking he must have gone inside to play with his toys in his chest. He wasn't there either. I looked back at the window and noticed how odd the blinds were hanging. I hadn't noticed it before, so I pulled the blinds back, and there he was laid out below on the ground. I screamed so loud my daughter came running out of her bedroom. I told her Izaiah had fallen out the window and to go downstairs. I had to get my shirt on. I grabbed my shirt and ran down the stairs while putting my shirt on, realizing all in that moment that she probably shouldn't see him. Somehow, I made it down right behind her. I told my daughter to run to the leasing office and tell them to call 911 because Izaiah fell out of the window. While picking him up from the grass. I instantly called out to God in prayer and ran with him to the office. The young ladies in the office were already on the phone, and I asked them to ask the operator to tell me what I should do. Should I be holding him? The operator instructed to have me lie him down on the ground. I just kept praying for him while waiting for help to arrive. They asked if they could call anyone else for me, I said yes, my children's momma, who was one of my aunts who raised me. I spoke briefly with her, telling her "The Boy" (one of his nicknames) had fallen out of his bedroom window and that I was waiting for the ambulance so we can get him to the hospital. I explained I would call her later to meet us there. It was in that moment that I realized that all I had was my faith.

You see, the Sunday before this unforgettable Friday was Mother's Day. We were at church getting ready for a week-long revival of amazing preachers from all over. That Mother's Day was so special to me. My kids and I were dressed in yellow. It was a beautiful Sunday service. I was just proud to be their mom. Izaiah knew he was handsome on this particular day. He literally walked inside of the children's church with little assistance. He had a little spring peacoat on, and he walked in with the most confidence I've ever seen in a two-year-old without a care in the world. He literally hugged and kissed us bye without a glance back. After church, I wanted to go have some studio pictures taken of us. Nothing too fancy—just over at the nearby mall in the photo studio. But I went home and made my family Mother's Day dinner and enjoyed a lovely spring day with them. It was the perfect Mother's Day. Looking back, I wish I had followed my gut instinct to take the pictures. The week of revival was just what I needed to build up my faith. I fell in love with God in a real way. I was excited with my development in my walk with God. I felt renewed, restored, and so hopeful. I learned during this week in particular to always pray over my children while speaking blessings over their life. I'd been to many conferences before, but I was just in awe of God and his many blessings in my life. I was on my way. Life was going to be everything I had imagined and so much more, simply because of my love for God. It was just what my soul needed and I felt new in Christ. I had no idea how my faith was going to get tested in the days to come.

My son was rushed to the hospital. I rode with him in the ambulance, quoting all of the scriptures I knew, praying, and just walking by faith and not by sight, because, in my right mind, there was no way in hell my son was going to walk away and be the same from falling out of a third-floor window. But I believed the God who had blessed me yesterday would do it again for my son on that day. I just believed and prayed. They flew my son to another hospital where they would take better care of him. I kept telling God, "Thank you, and yes, you are a healer." Although, I wasn't an official member of the church I had been attending, I called them for prayer, and not only did they pray, but the pastor also met us at the hospital. My family and now my church family were all in the waiting area, praying for a miracle. We held prayer vigils in that waiting room expecting God to show us signs and wonders of his love for my family. We desperately needed a miracle—one I was sure we would get.

Later that night, I was escorted to a room down a really long hall with several turns, telling me that I could only have a few family members present with me to speak some encouraging words to my baby to help get him through his next surgery. My sister, brother, and best friend walked with me, and I just remember how bright it was for it to be night. We finally got to our destination. The nurse walked out and said she would be right back with my baby. I was excited to see him and tell him how brave and strong he was and that he was such an amazing beautiful little boy. I had my whole speech ready to inspire him to fight. Out of nowhere, my brother said to me, "Mka, he's dead." I screamed at him, "Why the fuck would you say that?" with such hate for him in that moment because we didn't need that negative energy. I cried, "Why would you say that? He's not." My brother replied, "That's why they brought you here. He didn't make it." I cried and fought him. He held me tight, and I just wanted him to be the biggest liar. A few seconds later, someone came in saying they were so sorry for my loss. He didn't make it. As I write this, I'm still bothered and full of tears by this moment. I felt like they should have given me another chance to see him alive before they rolled him into that room to me already dead. I couldn't believe that my brother understood that the long walk was the walk to tell me he was gone. I was devastated. I screamed over and over, "No! No! No! Why, God? Why!?" When I finally saw him, I instantly knew that it was just his body. His spirit was already gone. I would never be the same.

My son, Izaiah Lee Anthony Fair, died that night Friday, May 13, 2005. He was two years old. When he died, all of my dreams for him died as well. He was my only son, my prince who would never grow to become a king. I would not be able to drop him off at his first day of kindergarten. I would not be able to sit in the stands and be his biggest cheerleader. Even at the age of two, he loved everything sports. He watched ESPN faithfully with his dad. He would also recreate the moves with his big cousins. I would no longer be able to hear him boss his big sister, Bi Bi, as he called her. Life after his transition was a big blur for many months.

This year, 2020, my son would have been a senior in high school. I mostly remember him as my toddler. If you were to meet me now, and before hearing this story, you would know me as a girl mom. What you would know if we became personal enough is that I once raised a little prince on this side of heaven. He is with me every day. I may not mention him, but I'm very aware of his presence. I know my angel's name. Sometimes he comes to me as a monarch butterfly, other times, in a story from my two youngest daughters who were born ten years after him. I believe it was my angel who introduced me to my current husband. After all, my husband was born on the same day that my little prince died. He's the reason why I am now the mother of my two little girls.

When my son left and was reunited with God, I kept telling God, "I don't know why you think I can handle this, because I cannot," but I learned in my darkest moments to just trust Him with my whole heart. I had nothing left in me. I was heartbroken. Literally. I used to hold my chest because it felt like the pain was too much. I kept asking God, "How can I live without him? Am I even supposed to?" Of course, I still had my princess who needed me, but I was such a mess. I just couldn't take the pain of not being able to be his mommy anymore. So I had to have a real talk with God. I said, "Listen here, God, if you can take this hurt away, then maybe I can live." I believe over the days, weeks, and then months and years to come, the holy spirit did just that. I read my Bible and started to remember whose child I was. I was hopeless, yet hopeful, because the more I got into the word and the more spirit guided me, the more I began to see my life being whole again. It was painful to let go of the pain. There were days where I would have joy and then mentally beat myself up, because how was I supposed to smile again? I was supposed to grieve until I saw my son again, right? It was crazy how I felt being happy meant dishonoring my son in a strange way. I started to read everything that gave me hope—Joel Osteen's books and *The Secret* by Rhonda Byrne. I started creating vision boards. I just started to view everything from a different perspective. My life began to change. I expected blessings daily, and they would appear. I read the Book of Job, and I began to tell God that I wanted my story to be like Job's. I wanted double for my trouble. I am here seventeen years later with double for my trouble.

God hears all of your prayers. I met the man of my dreams, and even though my tubes were tied, I was able to have two more children through in vitro fertilization. So in my current life, I have a grown daughter, a son who's in the spirit realm, and two amazing little ladies. I am so blessed that God blessed me beyond all that I could have imagined. The minute I let go and let God and pursued life with no limits, everything unfolded in such a divine way. I just became a vessel. The spirit guided my every step, and it's never failed me. My current husband's born date is my son's death date—May 13. The day I thought would forever be the worst day of my life is now a day that we all celebrate.

I hope my story inspires you to never give up. God comes to give us life and life more abundantly. Just keep living. Stay in tune to your creator. Walk by faith and not by sight. It will all work out in the end if you give your heart to the one who created you. You are so loved. To anyone reading this book, know that your best is yet to come. I'm so thankful that I never gave up on my darkest day, and I encourage you to stay the course through faith. God's promise will get you through. I know because it happened for me, not because I'm so great, but simply because I believed He would.

Mirror Images

NICOLE CURRY

Have you ever looked at your reflection in the mirror and found that you no longer recognize the person staring back at you? There was something different and *not* in a good way. You didn't look like yourself nor could you identify with yourself anymore. Almost nothing made sense as you stood there in the mirror seeking solutions. Kind of like waiting for your internal navigation system to finish rerouting to direct you to a place of clarity. Desperate to get back to a time before you were left with far more questions than answers.

"How could this be happening?

"Why me?

"Lord, how could You do this to me?!"

"Aren't I a good person?"

Those were just *some* of the questions on constant replay in the recesses of my mind and hollows of my heart. Being a woman had been hard. Being a young woman diagnosed infertile had been downright brutal. I wondered what I had done to possibly deserve that. I had always been taught that God would never leave or forsake me, just like it says in Deuteronomy 31 Verse 8. If that were true, why did I feel so *empty*, so *useless* as a woman, and so *alone*? It had been easy to hold fast to my beliefs when everything was going well, but what about when sickness came? Well, I quickly became angry and bitter believing God had let me down. Didn't God spare His children from that type of pain? I had a lot to learn, much of it the hard way. Eventually, I'd come to understand that if I endured the very same pain I once viewed as punishment, it could also be transformed into power.

To quote a dear friend, Ty H., "Warriors are born through opposition; trailblazers are raised in obscurity." Today I pen this chapter as both warrior and trailblazer for anyone amidst a life-altering diagnosis, chronic illness, or *any* challenge. Everyone has their own journey, and this one is mine. A journey that began with an infertility diagnosis but certainly did not end there.

I remember February 6, 2011, like it was yesterday. The morning of my follow-up appointment with my gynecologist. "No big deal," I thought. I was proven terribly wrong. It's not every day that your doctor tells you that your body won't permit you to do what a woman is designed to do by nature—bear children. Endometriosis, adenomyosis, fibroid tumors, and polycystic ovarian syndrome (PCOS) were the culprits. I'd been formally diagnosed by a specialist whom I had consulted as a second opinion because I found the first doctor I saw less than thorough. I was assured this time around yet angered. I was grateful for his level of expertise, but my heart was broken. All over the place emotionally, I sat there trying to listen attentively while my doctor explained everything in detail. I remember feeling drained before I eventually went numb. I would really grow to embrace the numbness I felt. A little too much to be honest.

I don't remember much after leaving my doctor's office that day, it's all a blur. My hopes and dreams of possibly having a child of my own one day had been taken away just like that. Age 34 at the time, I was a little older than most but still younger than some moms. Not to mention the guy I was dating at the time was adamant about wanting a family. "Well I guess that's over!" I thought rather absentmindedly to myself. "No need in prolonging the inevitable." This wasn't fair. No longer numb, I was starting to feel horrible all over again, and I didn't want to feel anything at all if I could help it. Talking about it was simply out of the question.

Over the next few weeks and months, I was beginning to experience the reactionary highs of "I'm strong! I can handle this!" and lows of "Lord Jesus! What is the point of it all?" So many emotions were flooding me at warp speed. I cried so many tears in secret. I thought surely I'd drown. At times I felt like I might collapse any minute from the weight of the sadness. I had no idea how to *live* with a problem this big that couldn't be fixed. What was worse, I didn't know if I wanted to.

While I *still* loved the Lord, I was angry with Him because I believed He'd done this *to* me. How could I trust in His goodness after something this bad had happened? In hindsight, I can see where that belief system prevented me from unburdening my heart and giving over my troubles to Him. I ended up carrying them and hurting myself in the process (literally and figuratively). At the time, all

I wanted to do was feel better *if* I had to feel anything at all. Enter multiple episodes of reckless binge drinking and the repeated recurrence of a very destructive coping mechanism from my younger days—cutting (self-harm).

For me, razor blades and blood were like a twisted tonic. Each cut gave me a sense of euphoria and a kind of sick release by providing an escape. I cut to numb my pain. I cut to control the intensity of my pain. At times, I cut just to feel alive. Eventually, I was cutting just to cut because I couldn't stop. It had become compulsory. What I was once able to start then stop at will, what I used to have control over was now controlling me. Self-harm *was* my drug of choice, and I was addicted, getting my "highs" from the endorphin release and hitting new "lows" each time I didn't engage. Trading pain for pain is tricky and isn't something I recommend. I found it better to face down my "inner demons" than to become them.

I thought I'd *try* reaching out to a few family or friends I figured I could trust. A *couple* of them were empathetic, but I was typically met with either outright pity or worse, unsupportive advice. On one notable occasion, I was told that I "just needed to pray harder for God to fix it...cuz ain't no man gonna want you if you can't have no babies!" It honestly felt more like an indictment and only added to my internal shame, worthlessness, and feelings of deficiency. Feeling more isolated and alone than ever, my destructiveness continued. My life (as I'd known it) had lost meaning and felt as though "Nicole" had faded away. Nothing *looked* out of place, but the truth was I had begun to confuse being numb with being invincible. I still worked every day, took care of my mother, and was a supportive auntie, the strong friend to many, and beloved godmother of one (at the time). It didn't matter if I got all of it done while heavily sedated under a dense fog of nothingness—did it? I wish I knew then what I know now—that there's a difference between existing vs. living.

Infertility had taken over my life. Everywhere I looked, there were constant reminders of what I would never be—a mother. At work in the laboratory, I was surrounded by pregnant women or women just like me, except better candidates for the in vitro fertilization process. Within my faith community, I worked diligently with the youth as a mentor and youth advocate. Post-diagnosis, though, I would be lying if I said working with youth and young adults was always easy despite how much I loved them. In my personal life, there was the added pressure of intrusive comments and insensitive questions: "No babies yet? Girl, you know your Mama is ready for some grandchildren!" "You better hurry up, get married, and have some babies. Time's running out!" It became easier for me to tell people that I didn't want children or just laugh right along with them. Nothing was funny though.

Before I knew it, three years had passed with me anesthetized on nothingness. Time flies when you're feeling numb, or rather living life on autopilot. That's the thing about traumatic life experiences—they can alter one's sense of space and time, or so I've learned. The fact is my despair had been real. My mental anguish was also very real. The depression had been dark, and I'd been tormented by suicidal ideations that seemed relentless. The truth was that I suffered greatly in that three-year period because my mental health was in jeopardy. Draped in excuses for why I refused to seek professional help, I chose to cover my bruised skin in long sleeves and wrist bands. I hid my heartache behind a fake smile and kept right on living out my brokenness.

It wasn't until late 2014 that I would see the pain of my infertility may actually have meaning, or better yet, purpose. A friend confided in me about the uncertainty of her fertility. I listened, uninterrupted to another woman speak about something with which I'd become intimately acquainted. She expressed a familiar sentiment of feeling completely isolated and alone. She felt like no one understood her struggle and her pain and that very few were even genuinely concerned. In that moment, I had a decision to make. I could let our encounter remain surface or allow the pain I'd been carrying bear fruit on *both* of our behalves by sharing my story with her. I believe my willingness to be open was the beginning of the shift: transforming the pain I had been feeling into power. I hadn't let go of all that troubled me, but I wasn't holding on to it as tightly either. I had come a long way being able to share but still had work to do in terms of my own healing. I've discovered that progress doesn't need to be linear in order for growth to occur. By the close of that year, I was mending, seeing a mental health professional, and on my way to stabilizing and truly coming to grips with my current diagnosis. In other ways, I was bracing for impact once again.

What was about to come might sound equally heart-breaking. No, it wasn't easy, but if I'd learned nothing else from what I'd already been through, it was this: perspective is key. On July 23, 2015, I was diagnosed with three very real, profoundly serious autoimmune diseases in the form of lupus, secondary rheumatoid arthritis, and antiphospholipid syndrome (APS). It was decision time again. Was I going to spiral out of control like I did once before? Or would I draw from my other experience, remember what did and did not work, stop with my brand of excuses, and try to do better?

Autoimmune diseases like lupus are difficult to explain. To oversimplify, my immune system is broken. Instead of making antibodies against foreign invaders, my immune also makes *autoantibodies* against its own cells, tissues, and organs. This can affect any system within my body, and the secondary conditions are an extension of that. Symptoms of each of these overlapping diseases are similar. Medication regimens are rigorous and medical appointments plentiful. Managing all of this is indeed a full-time job with no time off.

There is something to be said for being told that you were inching towards death's door that changes your personal philosophy on life and living. It was like someone turned the power back on or reconnected me to my power source. In the absence of church building, preacher, or altar, God and I were reconciled on the exam table in my rheumatologist's office. He had been there all along, waiting on me to trust Him even from the bottom of my heartache. I just needed to decide to fight and continue to utilize the tools I learned over the years in therapy. I'd come to the realization that my mental health was just as important as my physical and spiritual health was.

Over the course of these past five years living with autoimmune diseases, I've discovered a different caliber of strength—*His strength,* made perfect in my weakness (2 Corinthians 12:9). The thing about having lupus (and both secondary components) is I never know which system in my body it may attack next. The burden of "what if?" is much too big for me to carry, and so I learned quickly to give such matters over to God. I choose to be at peace and have found the practice of *mindfulness* helpful. Being present in the moment has really kept me from spiraling mentally when it comes to the uncertainty of these ailments. The symptoms of lupus range from mild to simply awful (for example, flares). There's no way to sugar coat that. It's tough. There are good days, bad days, and everything in between. Fortunately, I've remained largely independent and reasonably active and am currently working towards mastering the art of how not to overdo it. (Wish me luck!)

This time around, I didn't attempt to shut everyone out. I've learned that support—*real* support—is vital when going through a trial. I am grateful for my circle: my mother, my family (biological and extended), rock solid friends and four amazing godchildren. I've been blessed to *be* a blessing to others, only this time I'm paying it forward on a larger platform. In June of 2019, I was given the opportunity to be the featured guest on *The Donta Show ft. Dana* to discuss lupus and women of color. Out of that podcast, the Sistas of Strength (S.O.S.) Online Lupus Support Community was born. S.O.S. provides a safe space for those living with lupus and other chronic illnesses to openly discuss their struggles and triumphs with others who "get it." S.O.S. also provides information, advocacy and additional resources, particularly to those who have been recently diagnosed. It's an honor to champion this project with a stellar leadership team of four other amazing women. We welcome *anyone* who may be facing tough times, desires to feel less alone, or is looking for a semblance of community. Find us on Facebook. We'd love to connect with you.

I close this chapter from a position of humility, not perceived perfection. Let the record reflect I've gotten it wrong much more than I've gotten it right. May the next woman's journey be that much more bearable because of my transparency. The barely recognizable woman in mirror has at last been identified, and her name is *Conquerer*. Really, she is so much more. She's both woman as well as warrior; a butterfly representing hope and a wolf that embodies resilience. Her reflection in the mirror affirms that neither lupus nor infertility diminished a thing. Her value more intact, she knows she has much yet to learn and even more still to accomplish. No longer a stranger, the woman in the mirror is *me*.

Slowing Down in the Fast Lane

PAMELA LATHAN

On October 30, 1963 at approximately 11:00 am, God blessed my parents with their only daughter and my brothers with their only sister. My brothers continually asked my mom for a little sister. After 11 years, I finally hit the scene to meet my two brothers and my parents. My dad was a merchant seaman and later a machine operator at Con Edison, and mom was a stay-at-home wife/mother. My dad always wanted my mom present when we got home from school. Although we lived in the projects, we lived in the best five-room apartment. In 1978, my parents purchased a four-bedroom duplex co-op apartment on the Upper East Side of Manhattan. It was like a house inside an apartment. Most people had never seen an apartment like ours. We had moved on up like The Jeffersons, on to better living. My parents loved to entertain in our home. They would give dinner and birthday parties and invite everybody. I had a birthday party every year. Everyone would look forward to coming to our house, young and old, even when we lived in the projects.

Being raised with brothers who were 13 and 11 years older, plus older cousins and their friends, I was exposed to "mature situations." I ended up growing up pretty fast. I even walked at eight months. My advancement in life came with experiences I was actually too young to indulge in.

Since I didn't have any sisters, my girl cousins in New York and god sisters in Michigan were my sisters. Growing up was fun because I was able to split my time between the two. I spent most of my summers in Michigan with my god sisters. This is where I lost my virginity at 13—yes, 13. As I look at 13-year-old girls today, I truly acknowledge that I was being too damn grown trying to ride in the fast lane. I was 15 when my mom first learned of this. I thought she was going to kill me, but she was more understanding than I expected. She immediately made an appointment for me to get birth control. My fast life at that point really took off.

In 1977, I was accepted to Julia Richman High School in Manhattan. As a freshman, I was concentrating on making new friends and getting acclimated to my new freedom of "teenage adulthood." The first two girls I met turned out to be lifelong friends—one becoming my best friend into adulthood and beyond. Together, the three of us were known as the "Fly Girls." Others gave us that nickname because we dressed in the fliest gear—Jordache, Gloria Vanderbilt, Sergio Valente designer jeans, and the best footwear in shoes, sneakers or boots. Our hair was always tight, and we got the attention of all the boys—cute ones and not so cute ones. We definitely had our options.

Hanging with these two young ladies wasn't enough for me. I had to find some more friends with whom to be popular. Little did I know these were the friends from whom I should have stayed away. I made the decision not to follow my good friends to class. Instead, I followed the bad friends. I began cutting class and getting high. Weed and cocaine were our preferred drugs. Although my two besties hung out sometimes, they knew when to go to class.

High school was not the first time I experimented with drugs. I started smoking weed in junior high school, but in high school I had my first experience with cocaine. Again, fast lane living. I always thought I was grown. Because of my height and maturity, many others thought I was grown too, and I knew to use it to my advantage.

My first semester of being a sophomore, I failed everything. I had seven or eight classes, and all had the same red grade, F. I even failed P.E. Now that was really pathetic. I knew my mom was going to kill me, and she almost did. She made sure that when I returned after the Christmas break I had a new outlook on life. So since I wanted to live, I went back with my besties who went to class and left the others alone. I was knocked back into the reality that I wasn't grown at all.

The choices I made to hang out with the wrong crowd were very costly when it was time to graduate. I was supposed to graduate with my Fly Girls in June of 1981 but had to endure an extra term. My senior year, I went to night school twice a week taking English, and guess what else? Gym! Although I completed all requirements by January, I couldn't graduate until June 1982. I didn't even attend the graduation ceremony. My Fly Girls were gone, and it wasn't the same. Plus, I was working full time and didn't want to go. Here I was, the baby and only girl in the family, and I had robbed my parents of seeing me walk the stage to get my diploma.

I followed my best friend to Bernard Baruch College and started college more mature—or so I thought. Baruch was considered to be one of the best city colleges at that time in New York City, but I had a hard time adjusting there. My best friend was smarter than me (hell it seemed as though everyone there was smarter than me). She had good grades in high school, which helped qualify her for better classes at Baruch. I tried to fit in but didn't feel like I did. I had mediocre grades and had to take all remedial classes my first year. It was like being back in high school again. I continued to party and not focus on school. Still growing up too fast.

By my sophomore year, it wasn't happening for me there. I began to relive my high school experiences and started failing again. At first, I said "what the hell," because I had received grants paying for me to go to school, plus a little extra in my pocket. I knew my parents would be disappointed again by me failing. They always instilled in us the importance of getting a good education, especially my dad. With only a high school diploma, he was very educated in most subjects as though he was a college scholar. He used his self-taught knowledge to build a successful tax preparation business and offered advice to many family and friends.

In September of 1984 I became a student at Fashion Institute of Technology (FIT). This school was very trendy and birthed many top designer alumni and fashion-related professionals in the industry. Since being a former model, I was better acquainted with this industry and thought it would be a great experience. I loved it at FIT. Although I wished I could draw and become a famous designer, I took the other option of fashion buying and merchandising. My good grades were a great boost to my ego and confidence. I was slowing down and making smarter decisions with maturity and life was back on track.

During the second semester, I was working full time for the Immigration and Naturalization Service as Assistant Supervisor in the Trial Attorney Division and going to FIT part time at night. I suddenly began to experience major lower back pains. The pain was so excruciating and caused me to have problems walking. I continued to work and go to school until one day I wasn't able to urinate. My mom already knew I was having the back problems, but when I wasn't able to urinate, she took me to the hospital. We took a cab to one of New York City's well known East Side hospitals. They examined and catheterized me and sent me home, advising if I didn't use the bathroom to come back. My lower back pain was getting to be unbearable and walking was very difficult. One evening, I had taken a cab home, and by the time I got home I was almost crawling. After three times back and forth at that same hospital and no change, I went to Lenox Hill Hospital. I was catheterized first, followed by some x-rays and a CT scan. They could not determine what was going on with me but knew they could not let me go home. I was admitted that night after walking into the hospital and woke up not being able to walk at all.

I tried standing and almost fell on the floor. I immediately started screaming. The nurse came in, and I told her I could not feel my legs and almost fell out of the bed. She tried to help me and noticed the same thing I did—I could not walk. She called for a doctor and told him what was going on. He began to examine me by touching my toes asking me if I could feel his touch. I said no. I could see him wiggling my big toe, but still could not feel his touch. He then moved up to one calf. He used this silver object in his hand and he had this bewildered look on his face. Naturally he didn't want to share his observation, but after an MRI, the confirmed diagnosis was transverse myelitis (damage to the myelin sheath that covers the spinal nerves), and just like that, I was paralyzed from my waist down for 52 days.

I spent half the time recovering medically, and then off to rehab to be taught how to walk again. My mom was by my side every day, morning to night. Dad, on the other hand, came once and a while and would stay a quick five minutes. When he got ready to leave, I would say to him "Dad, you're leaving already?" He would say, "Yes, Pamela. hospitals are not my bag." Realizing the real reason why he didn't stay, I would say, "Okay, Daddy. See you soon." He couldn't stand seeing his little girl in that condition. To this day, I still have incontinence issues and lack control of some functions, but God blessed me with the use of my limbs once again. With extensive outpatient therapy, I successfully moved from wheelchair to walker to cane to being able to strut my stuff once again without assistance.

Although being paralyzed was a very bad experience for me, the day I lost by dad was by far the worst day of my life. He passed on May 4, 2004, two days before his 75th birthday, after years of suffering from emphysema. He was hospitalized on St. Patrick's Day. I will never forget my mom calling saying my dad asked her to cook the traditional meal of corn beef and cabbage. When it was time to eat, mom noticed he was gasping for breath. By this time, the oxygen he had been using for years was no longer effective. This was the first time in his life that he actually said "I want to go to the hospital."

He was hospitalized on Wednesday night, March 17. My husband and I went to visit him the next morning before going to work. Dad seemed okay. He was sitting up talking and was breathing on his own. After we left, I had no idea that would be my last conversation with him. The doctor called stating my dad had breathing problems through the night and had been placed on a ventilator. Not being familiar with this, I didn't know what to expect. I left work, and we headed to the hospital. I walked in and saw my dad with all these tubes from the ventilator. I immediately did not get a good feeling looking at him like that, but the doctor tried to ease our concerns by saying, "It looks worse than it is." Over the next 48 days, we watched my dad rapidly deteriorate, and finally, he was gone from us.

I thank my parents for making it comfortable for me to stay at home until I was 34—yes, 34. Why move out when I had it so good? My mom was there to cook for me, wash my clothes, make up my bed, and clean up my room. Living at home allowed me to buy three new cars as an adult and eventually have good credit to purchase a three-family house with my brothers.

Once I was out on my own, I was able to live the single life in my own apartment. I think men were intimidated by my height, beauty, and confidence. That is, until the love of my life entered only nine months later. As I was looking for love in all the wrong places, he was right under my nose. Born and raised in the same church organization but in separate cities, we found each other in 1998, moved in together in 1999, and married in 2002. I'm grateful my dad was able to walk me down the aisle to give my hand to my husband. Life did not afford us children together, but I was blessed with his three beautiful daughters and now three beautiful granddaughters.

Both my husband and I were working and doing very well. My husband was working for a university, and I owned a successful salon. I wanted for nothing. If I wanted something, I bought it. I didn't even need to look at the price tag. As we were thriving, life happened and things changed. We were forced to close our salon, then my husband lost his job. We were both unemployed together for almost two years. We exhausted our unemployment, our savings, our 401ks, our stock, and our retirement funds. We struggled and often times were embarrassed by our situation, but the God of Israel prevented us from hitting rock bottom. We held our faith and he didn't let us fall.

Although I steered off into some pretty destructive behaviors, God stuck with me and brought me back. I was met with many adversities early in my life and managed to overcome it all. From losing my virginity to experimenting with drugs at a very young age, from failing in school to being paralyzed and then stripped financially from head to toe. It's by the grace of God I'm here to share my story of triumph and victory.

I am thankful to our family who prayed for and supported us and this gracious God we serve. We are on the road of recovery. My husband was offered the position of Professor of Practice/Director of Online Learning at the University of San Diego in September of 2019, and I am returning to my human resources roots as a consultant.

Slowing down in the fast lane gave me the opportunity to appreciate and value the blessings God had given me, from family to good health. Now I'm ready to journey on, reaping some of those rewards God promised me. I'm grateful and looking forward to more blessings as we live our best lives in sunny California.

Potential and Purpose

REGINA WEATHERSPOON-BELL

I lost my mom at age 12. I ended a bad marriage at age 28 (lasted 2 years from vows to divorce). I lost my only biological (baby) brother when I was 33. At 33 years old, I was told I most likely would not be able to have kids. Then I was faced with a major career change at 40 without the benefit of a degree.

It was all of the above and more that prepared me to become a woman. I am living and learning to live in the fullness of my potential and purpose. I have a career that affords me to serve people daily in a meaningful way. As a businesswoman, exciting opportunities, amazing projects, and relationships are a huge part of my work and joy. Being a wife, mother, daughter, sister, aunt, and friend are my biggest blessings. Often, I think that if it had not been for the grace of God and my belief in the constant thought that I was created to be and do more, oh my, what a life I would have lost and missed out on.

My truth is simple. Yes, Jesus loves me. If not for Him, I would not have this opportunity to speak life, love, and joy to you. At a very young age I realized there was something in me that I wanted to do. I was creative. I loved music, literature, art and dance. I loved the art of conversation, discussion, and debate. I was a listener and a thinker. I was also insightful and wise for my age (at least that's what some of the elders of my family told me). I was also smart and loved school. However, it wasn't until I was a grown woman facing divorce, financial instability, and finally coming face to face with deep personal childhood insecurities that I started to find out and learn what I was made of. I was grown when I realized there was a purpose for me and that God had already placed all the potential inside of me to make it happen

I was 13 years old when I first realized that God truly loves me. The loss of a parent at any age can be devastating, but as a young girl entering puberty—can you imagine? This was also the first time I can remember experiencing jealousy, envy, and pettiness, not only among girls but also among adult women, who were negative and just mean spirited. I don't remember before my mom's passing being exposed to grown adult women who were not loving and kind. These women told me that I would never be anything. It was predicted that I would be pregnant and on drugs by age 15. Really?! Well, none of that false prophecy came true, thank God! The damage was done, though. It would be years before I realized how much and how deep my self-doubt and insecurities ran. It would also be years before I allowed myself to truly grieve the loss of my mother and come to grips with the huge responsibility she placed on me by saying, "If something happens to me, you are to take care of your father and raise your brother."

I had always been told be careful what you pray for. I prayed to God to give me who I thought was the man of my dreams. He was exceptionally talented, wrote and arranged music, played a variety of instruments, and also produced. His talent was seductive, and I was hooked. He had charisma, and when he was on, he was on! The hardcore truth was that he loved himself and he loved that I loved him, but he didn't love me. I was dependable and loyal and fed his ego. I was safe, but he absolutely was not in love with me. So our relationship came to an end. Even in the heat of desperately loving him, there was something in me that said, "You deserve more. There is more to true love and respect than this." The truth in realizing he was not in love with me was devastating. I was young, broken, insecure, abandoned, and anxious, feeling unsure if I could make it through the next minute.

I allowed myself to believe that my value was in him. What was so wrong with me that I was not lovable and valuable to me? The truth is it wasn't all me. He had some responsibility and accountability, but I had taken on total responsibility for the success of our relationship. Once I accepted the truth in the fact that he didn't love me like I loved him, God placed healing in my life, and slowly but surely, I moved on to being better not bitter. I am grateful for the experience that made me decide what kind of woman I was going to be. I chose to become a whole woman, a grown woman, and the hard work was just beginning. I didn't realize at that time that womanhood is ever-evolving, but the core lesson of learning to love and value yourself is where it begins.

Heartbreak and disappointment are as much a part of life as joy and happiness. The challenge is how we process and navigate the experience. It's an understanding that we determine and choose how to be whole and happy, even during the times of great pain and challenge. What I learned early on is that for me, the truth (good, bad, or indifferent) is essential to my happiness.

I may never know why the love of my life, my best friend, and my brother—the person who knew my frailties and all but loved me anyway—left me. Barry is my younger (we are three years apart) and only biological brother. He died in 1991 from AIDS at the age of 30. When he was first diagnosed, I asked God if he was going to make it, and if not, to please prepare me to walk this walk with him on this side of life being the best sister I could be. God let me know that he wasn't going to come out of this alive. So for the time we had left together, we laughed, we cried, we sang and danced, we revisited our childhood memories, we spoke our truths, and we promised to always hold each other close in our hearts no matter which side of life we were on. Our theme song is Patti Labelle's *You Are My Friend*.

To say it was incredibly hard to let Barry go falls so short of the truth. One night, a few months after his passing, he came to me in a dream and he told me it was "time for me to let him go and get on with my life." All I can say is that from that point on, I began making a life for me. I slowly let go of the subconscious weight of my mother's instructions to be responsible for my father and my brother. I realized that my young interpretation of what she said I had taken literally. I had sacrificed knowing me, my wants, and my desires because I believed my responsibility was to be a caretaker of others. My value and worth were in others. Of course, I have never let my brother go, but he gave me the beautiful gift of liberation by encouraging me to let go and get to know me, live life for me. Thank you, my beautiful brother, for your truth in love!

On February 14, 1992, I married my husband, and two years later we were blessed by me giving birth to our precious son. Our son not only looks like my brother, but he acts like his Uncle Barry in many ways. I thank God for giving me back a little of Barry through my son. I also thank God for the wonderfulness and joy of my son.

I may never know why when I was 12 years old, my mother, who loved and nurtured me, who taught me to believe that I could do and be whatever I put my mind to, was taken away. What I do know is that she was an incredibly smart, beautiful, compassionate, and talented Black woman who placed in me principles of strength that I still use today. She gave me a father who never let me go. He raised me and my brother. My dear dad continues to love, challenge, and support me.

I've learned that it's not always what you lose, but what you gain. I've learned it doesn't matter what others think of you, it's what you know of yourself. I knew at 40 years old that my life wasn't over and that I had good work to accomplish and visions to turn into my reality. So having to leave an industry (entertainment management) I loved and worked in for almost 20 years and reinvent myself without a college degree was daunting. There were many who took the opportunity to try and make me feel small because I did not have a college degree. "What do you think you can do?" many of them asked. I was a 40-year-old Black woman with no degree, a husband, a son, a mortgage and a car note. The questions continued. "What you gonna do?" "Who gonna hire you?" I knew that if I didn't face my fears and place my trust in a God who had given me everything I needed to move forward in purpose and power, I would never know the extent of my powerful mind and spirit.

Eventually I faced my fears, and life as I had envisioned it had become my beautiful reality. I am a business owner, a founder and CEO of a multi-cultural nonprofit organization, a business development consultant, a special event production planner, and a filmmaker. In addition, over the past eight years, I've had the privilege to serve as a Deputy Director to an elected official who's been committed to truly serving the people. I have received several humbling honors and recognitions for my work and service to women, children, and my community. I've been invited to sit as a member on some impressive boards and commissions. Despite all that I have achieved and acquired, I am most grateful that I never stopped believing I had a purpose.

I hope that sharing some of the sources of my insecurities, my feelings of being lost and without purpose yet feeling there's something more to me, and my feelings of "I just need to get to it" resonates with you if that's where you are finding yourself. I also hope that my resilience and steadfast belief in God resonates with you. Here is a golden nugget of truth. If He could do it for me, He absolutely can do it for you.

The key is to accept the truth of where we are in our lives with knowing "I am moving past this." I am going to learn the lesson, grow, and be better because of the experience. I will not stay in this moment any longer than it takes me to learn the lesson. I always say there's no harm in having a pity party just don't stay too long at the party. You have got to move, get a plan, and be ever mindful of what you feed your mind, body, and spirit. Find your faith, then trust in it. Stand firm in it and just watch God go to work. Watch how He leads your mind and spirit to higher evolved levels of thinking, living, and being. Trust and believe in the fullness of your potential and purpose.

Every Man I Love, I Lose

SARAILEAH CASSANOVA

It all started with my dad, the very first man I ever loved. He was my first superhero and this little girl's biggest fan. Being the only girl and having a mom with emotional hang-ups, insecurities, and bipolar tendencies was difficult. No matter how hard it was, I had my dad. He was my first Mr. Everything, and most importantly, the first man who ever loved me.

I have an older brother who loves me to pieces and a twin brother who loved me as well. We came into this world together with an unbreakable bond, but sibling love isn't the same as what my father shared with his little girl. My parents had a very volatile marriage, and my mom was very abusive to my dad. After trying for years to make things work, he decided to file for divorce, and that's where the losses began to take place in my life.

The divorce happened rather quickly. My father was granted custody of me and my twin. My eldest brother, from a previous marriage, would stay with my mother. Upset by the outcome, my mom packed up everything and abducted us, violating the custody order. She changed our names, altered our identities, and relocated to Los Angeles. With no real stability, we were constantly moving to multiple neighborhoods and changing schools.

As my father frantically searched for us, my mom would eventually tell us he was dead. We were lied to at six years old, but she was our mom. Why wouldn't we believe her?

Over the next few years, absolutely nothing could prepare me for the series of events that would take place. Two years after relocating, my older brother, now eighteen, was serving a four-year prison sentence for robbing a bank. On our eighth birthday, my twin brother and I had a party. While playing, my brother was hit by a truck and killed on impact. In a matter of three years, I lost my father (whom I believed was dead), my eldest brother to incarceration, and now my twin brother to a tragic accident.

I had a job and bought myself a car when I was 15 even though I didn't have a license. I remember hearing rumors from classmates. They assumed I sold drugs because I had a car and wore nice clothes. While sitting in class one day, a detective came in and took me to the police station. My first thought was, "I'm dead meat. They know I've been driving without a license!" A police sergeant began questioning me about my father. I calmly answered his series of questions but wondered what was going on. A Hispanic woman with dark hair took control of the conversation and introduced herself as a private detective. She said she had been looking for us for almost ten years. I asked why. She replied she had been hired by my father to find us. I insulted her and became rude, telling them how stupid they were because my father was dead. Then suddenly, I heard his voice. I'll never forget the chill that came over my body when I heard it. He was on speaker phone and had been listening the whole time. He uttered "Leah, baby it's me. I love you. Where is your brother?" I was lost, shocked, and remained silent before screaming, "What kind of sick fucking joke is this?" After calming down and coming to terms with the fact that the voice I clearly recognized was my father's, I apologized and broke the news my twin brother was dead. "Dad, he was hit by a truck and has been gone for seven years. I'm really sorry, Dad!" Imagine being fifteen years old and having to tell your father that his firstborn son is dead. I'd never heard anyone sob so terribly in my life. I felt angry, hurt, confused, and betrayed. How could my mother have done this to us? She also robbed my father of saying goodbye to his son.

I was never the type to question or challenge my mother. I was taught it was forbidden to do so and that children who disobeyed their parents or backtalked were given a one-way first class ticket to hell. I also feared her more than anything in this world. In my hurt and anger, I mustered up the courage to ask her why she lied to us. Her response would be cruel and heartless. "I am a Black woman, and that white judge gave custody of my children to a white man because they were racist. Nevada is racist. I believe he would've hurt you both. That white man could have raped and killed you. What was I supposed to do? He never cared about you all. He never offered me a dime for you." I responded, "How the hell could he offer us anything if he couldn't find us or communicate with us? If you thought he'd hurt us, why did you marry him and have children with him? You just took his children and disappeared for years." I asked her why she lied to us about him being dead, and she said it was none of my business. I was a child and needed to stay in a child's place, and if I ever questioned her again she would ship me off to boarding school. That was the first time in my life I had ever experienced hatred for my mother. I truly felt like a motherless child, unloved, and I just wanted to flee from her presence.

I began visiting my father under court order in Nevada. He still had custody and could have taken me from my mother, but he opted for visitation because he didn't want to change my way of life or put me through any more emotional or mental trauma. He was now remarried and had another son—my younger brother. By this time, I was sixteen years old, and he was nine years old. I loved being a big sister and was always excited to see my little brother and spend time with him. He was the most vibrant kid and absolutely fearless. As time progressed, the visits became more frequent, but the fun started to take a turn for the worse. My stepmother would blame me for things I didn't do and get upset if I didn't clean or do things her way. My father and I began to disagree as his new wife would attempt to discipline me for not being cooperative. After all, I was a headstrong sixteen-year-old who didn't know this woman from a can of paint. I barely knew my father. I was almost grown. She couldn't tell me anything, and she was certainly not about to run my life. My father chose his then wife and discontinued our relationship for the next four years. Once again, I was left feeling unloved, betrayed, and angry as hell. Just like that, I had lost my dad for the second time and lost the new relationship with my brother as well.

By the time I was 18, I was a college student driving a brand new car and had my own apartment. I had an amazing job and was well on my way to success. I felt accomplished and was very proud of myself. Within a year, I had been given a promotion at work, I was doing well in school, and I was feeling unstoppable. Two days before my nineteenth birthday, I ran into a young man I had known from childhood. He was handsome and sweet and had the most beautiful smile I had ever seen. I've always been a sucker for smiles. He was smart and funny, and had all the same goals as me. He was a hard worker, had a great job and a nice car, and lived on his own.

From the first day we reconnected, we had chemistry. Every day after that, we were together. We were a happy little couple living worry free and deeply in love for what we thought love was at nineteen years old. After dating and living together for almost two years, I got pregnant. We were both scared and contemplated aborting. We weren't sure if we were ready for the responsibility of having a child. We were young, still working towards our goals, and started experiencing problems in our relationship. After discussing our feelings and weighing our options, we decided to keep our child. We were excited and did all we could to prepare ourselves to be awesome parents to our little one, and for a while, it made us stronger. Our relationship seemed to be getting better.

In March 2004, I gave birth to a strong and healthy baby boy. He was eight pounds, four ounces and twenty-four inches long. He was a caramel-colored baby with a head full of jet-black hair and the biggest, most mysterious brown eyes. He was absolutely perfect. We jumped right into our roles of being mommy and daddy, and the adjustment came naturally. Being we were young parents, we had loads of energy, and the baby brought us lots of joy. As he began to grow, he met all of his milestones, and we were two proud parents. We had a happy, growing child who was surrounded with love, and we had a great support system to back us.

By the time our son was eighteen months old, things had taken a horrible turn in our relationship. We could never agree about anything and argued about everything. There was no compromising. We both were too young, stubborn, and immature to even try. We both had the "my way or the highway mentality," and it became a major part of our demise. We both had been unfaithful, and the relationship had become both mentally and physically abusive. At one point during an argument, my son's father became so angry with me that he discharged a fire extinguisher while I was holding the baby. My son and I could barely breathe, and in that moment, I knew the relationship could no longer continue. We ended the relationship and parted ways right before our son's second birthday. I was now a single mom, scared of being left alone, and had just lost the first man with whom I'd ever been in love.

During the course of my relationship with my son's father, I had reconnected with my dad. He had gone through a divorce, and we worked to rebuild our relationship. He apologized and explained some of the issues that had occurred in his marriage as the result of finding me. Apparently, his wife was insecure, could never have children of her own, and had been feeling anxiety about helping him raise another child that wasn't hers. My little brother wasn't her child. His mother had passed when he was very little. Also, she was a white woman and wasn't very comfortable being around his Black child. I accepted his apology, and we were able to move forward in our bond-building process. It was very nice being able to watch my now 17-year-old "big little brother" talk about the things he wanted to do and give him advice. The greatest thing of all was I got my dad and little brother back!

My dad loved being a new grandpa. My son was his first grandchild, and he lovingly called my dad "Grampoo," which melted my dad's heart! He'd belt out a Santa Claus laugh every time my son called for him. It excited him thinking about teaching my son and brother to be wilderness men. He looked forward to fishing, hunting, and hiking with them. I had no interest in those things and was happy to send all three of them on their way. Sista girl didn't have time for that.

My fearless little brother was now a fearless 19-year-old who had become a semi-professional skateboarder. He and his friends constantly worked on their tricks and techniques. Their YouTube channel had a very good network of young adults who were supporting them as they were building a brand. One evening, my brother had been spending some time at a friend's house. It got late, and he decided to call it a night. He hopped on his skateboard and was riding to the bus stop. Riding alongside a dark golf course, he crossed the street without using the crosswalk and was hit by a truck, killing him instantly. At 19 years old, with such a bright future ahead of him, he was gone in the twinkling of an eye. I was at work when my dad called. He said "Leah, he's gone!" With the loss of my baby brother, I had once again lost a man I loved so much.

After so much loss, life seemed to be returning to normal. I had my dad, I was working, I was in a relationship, and I was co-parenting and raising a healthy active son. He was about to hit another milestone—turning five. I was planning a huge block party. This would be the party to remember, and life was on the right track. Two months before my son turned five, I received the call no parent should ever receive. My son had been hospitalized and was clinging to life, and his father, my first love, had passed. I rushed to be by my baby's side. Having no time to process what happened, the doctors explained that I had to make a decision for my son who was on life support with no positive vitals. I held his hand, kissed his face, and expressed my love as I said goodbye. Every man I had ever loved, I lost, but my baby never got a chance to become a man.

Loss is hard and finding the strength to move forward is even harder. When you are right there with the pain, you can barely see your way out of it. You never get over losing people so close to you. The pain is relentless, and your tears seem never ending. Over time, it does become manageable. People say to stay strong, and part of that strength is trusting when you need a moment to be with your thoughts and feelings. Sometimes the healing starts again. I continue to manage through prayer, meditation, and healthy mourning. This has allowed me the space to endure and maintain my sanity. With the right support and grace from God, we can navigate through life even while hurting and attempting to heal. I will forever love and be grateful for the men whom God gave me and the time I had with them. Love is everlasting, even when it is stolen from you in the physical. Spiritually, love and your loved ones are always with you. I know that mine are with me.

Keep Pushing

SEANTE GLASS-FLOWERS

I was born Grandma's baby because my mother and father were teenage parents. My birth mom left me at the fragile age of three days old to return to Pittsburgh, Pennsylvania to be with my father. Convinced that she was too young to be a mom, she left me with my grandmother (whom I call mom) to be raised. As a child, I remember always being told that I was abandoned at birth, that my parents didn't want me, and that I was going to be just like my birth mother, who was now on drugs, had become a kleptomaniac, and was constantly going to jail. Those words would pierce my tender soul like a knife. I didn't understand why they would say those things about me. I had never done anything that could make them even think that of me. Why did they hate me so much? As I got older, I realized that it was because I was my grandmother's favorite child. She loved me, and I loved her. She loved to cook, and I loved to learn. I could do no wrong in her eyes. I was the perfect child. I used my grandmother's view of me as leverage as I got older. She would believe anything I said. Once I became a teenager, that trust was broken.

I got pregnant on my 15th birthday. History had repeated itself. I was going to be just like my mother. I had

no desire to be a mother. I was just young and dumb
listening to my friends who were having sex. I was just trying to escape the mental abuse I was receiving at home.
I wasn't trying to make a baby. I didn't want a baby, so
I had an abortion. This made my grandmother look at
me in a way she had never looked at me before. It was
a look of pure disgust. I was called a murderer. My aunts
would call the house and scream, "Murderer! Murderer!
Murderer!" through the phone. I felt alone and depressed
and sometimes wondered if I was really a murderer. Soon
after having the abortion, my grandmother purchased a
house in Lancaster, California. I hated everything about
Lancaster—the school, the heat, and the people. I could
not live there. So, I made the decision to go live with my
birth mom. She was fresh out of jail with a new boyfriend,
and I could go to Westchester High School. I had ruined
the relationship I had with my grandmother. I could not
take the way she looked at me. I was no longer perfect
in her eyes.

Living with my birth mom was challenging from the
start. She was verbally and mentally abusive. Constantly
being put down and made fun of, I questioned my decision to come live with my mom. I missed life before 15.
I never wanted for anything. Living with my mom was
totally different. She would have these really bad mood
swings even for something as simple as coming home and
not smelling Pine-Sol, meant the house wasn't clean. I began pouring Pine-Sol in the door jam so when she would
open the door she could smell it. To my surprise, she had
not completely changed her life. She was still stealing. I

remember taking a trip to the mall with my mom, and she told me not to follow her into the store. I watched through the window as she put what looked like a whole rack of baby clothes in her bag. I figured it was only a matter of time before she would get caught and end up back in jail.

After constantly being called a bitch and a whore by my birth mom, I felt less than, unloved, and unwanted. As older men started to show interest in me, it made me feel special. I felt wanted. To hold on to that feeling, I began dating a much older man. By senior year in high school, my birth mom was back in jail, and I was living with my 25-year-old boyfriend. The word on the streets was that I would be pregnant before the school year was over and that I would not graduate from high school. I was determined to prove them all wrong, and I did by walking the stage and not becoming pregnant.

After high school, I decided I wanted to become a chef. I had developed a passion and love for cooking after all those years cooking with my grandma. I got accepted to Le Cordon Bleu Culinary Arts Institute in Pasadena, California. The cost was a whopping $80,000. I needed a parent to cosign my loan. Both of my parents told me no. Devastated to say the least, I was not going to let them stop me. I began modeling to save up the money I needed for culinary arts school. Shortly after beginning my modeling career, I became pregnant. After having my son and now being called a plus-size model, I put modeling on the back burner and began working for the city of Los Angeles. After the birth of my daughter, I felt the burning desire to become a chef again, but I was still too young to get the loan on my own. Now as a married woman, that kind of debt with two small children made my dream of becoming a chef seem impossible. Until I found Los Angeles Trade Technical College.

I thrived in culinary arts school. Everything came naturally to me, and I was at the top of my class. My grandmother was once again proud of me, and graduation was around the corner. I did it. My hard work was paying off. My grandmother suffered a massive stroke that left her on kidney dialysis. I knew one of her dreams was to see me become a chef. Being the oldest of eleven siblings, my grandmother didn't get to go to college. She married my grandfather at the tender age of 15. With her being ill, I attended culinary arts school with no breaks to accelerate my graduation date. Then out of the blue, my grandmother died. Nothing could have ever prepared me for that moment. I had just spoken to her the day before. She was fine. I felt the wind was knocked out of my sail. I felt naked, exposed to the world. How could the only person who loved me be dead? And she died before she could see me become a chef.

Completely heartbroken and devastated with the loss of my grandmother, I became pregnant with my third child. How was I going to be able to pick up 50-pound pots of stock pregnant? What if my chefs found out? I would have to leave school. I went to my doctor and told him my dilemma. With my first pregnancy, I was on bed rest for seven months, so I was always terrified that could happen with this pregnancy. I did not want to be put on bed rest with graduation just a few weeks away. My doctor told me it was safe to continue what I had been do-ing. So here I was, unexpectedly pregnant with morning, noon, and night sickness and grieving my grandmother with finals around the corner. The only thing I wanted to do was lie in my bed and cry. My plans to graduate, go to Las Vegas, and work as a chef to build my name and become a master chef had been shattered. Through-out culinary arts school, my chefs thought my goals were quite ambitious because most chefs did not have a family. The job of a chef is their life. You are required to spend 12 to 15 hours a day or more at work, and you can't miss work. You have to show up, and your reputation precedes you. How was I going to be able to do this with a new baby? But first things first. I had to finish what I started and graduate. I was determined to continue to make my dreams come true and my grandmother proud. I got up out of the bed and continued to go to school. I would blast Diana Ross's song, *I'm Coming Out* in my car on my way to school with tears rolling down my face. I would get to school, throw up in the bathroom across campus so no one would hear me, brush my teeth, put on a brave face, and go to class that started at 6:30 am. I was hell bent on keeping my pregnancy a secret. I continued to work hard and produce top grades with delicious food. Soon, gradu-ation day came, and I graduated with President's Honors from culinary arts school. I felt my grandmother's spirit with me. I became a chef, and she was proud.

I decided to open a catering business because I need-ed flexibility. My dream of going to Las Vegas had been put totally on the back burner. I couldn't leave my new baby for the long hours that would be required of me as a chef, so I birthed Enchante's Catering. I started out selling five-dollar meals to all my husband's friends and our neighbors. Soon, I was booking birthday parties, dinner parties, weddings, and even craft services for celebrities.

Throughout every adversity, I always found a way to keep moving forward and never let anyone or anything stop me from reaching my goals. As a child being told I was going to be just like my mother, those very words motivated me to become a woman who was nothing like her. My older boyfriend who everyone swore was going to get me pregnant and leave was married to me for 24 years. We would still be married, but cancer took him from me. That's another story that I'll tell you about later. Together, we raised three beautiful children. As a mother, I made sure that my children never felt the rejection I felt as a child. I loved them, nurtured them, and made sure they got the best education. I went on every field trip and never missed a game or practice. I never called them out of their names. I never used words like nigga, stupid, jipped dog (I still don't know what a jipped dog is) or a lazy sow to describe them. I fed them words of encouragement and affirmations and love. I was determined to be a perfect wife, mom, and business owner.

When your kids become teenagers, you have the rude awakening that there's no such thing as a perfect mom. And when you fight with your husband, you understand that there's no perfect wife either. For years, I would overcompensate with my children, feeling the need to give them everything I didn't have. I soon learned that those were my hang-ups and not theirs. I had to learn that my children knew nothing about my upbringing. The only thing they knew was what I was teaching them. That's why Enchante's Catering became so important to me. It was a way for me to provide for my family, be there for my family, and to teach them hard work and determination. To never give up on their dreams. And I'm proud to say that it's working. My positive outlook in life has kept me going throughout the darkest times in my life.

Things were going well. I had a successful business, my kids were doing great in school, and my husband was loving and supporting me. Then cancer came into our lives and turned everything upside down. It swept through our lives and took everything—cars, savings, friends, and family. Very few people will stand by your side when you're at your lowest moments. You'll look around, and people to whom you've given your last won't even answer your calls. However, people whom you never thought would be there for you will show up.

I was walking three to seven miles a day looking for work because my husband could no longer provide for us, and without a car, catering was completely on the back burner. I hadn't worked for anyone for ten years, so at times, I felt like I had failed my family. We had no money. I had to ask my family for help, which was a very humbling experience. I had been on my own since I was 17 years old. How could I need help at the age I was now? I was so embarrassed. I put my pride aside and reached out to my family, who without any judgment came to my aid. I found a job that allowed me to support myself and continue to be caretaker for my husband until his passing on November 7, 2019. I buried him on November 11 and returned to work on November 14. I had to keep going. Life is for the living. I was really expecting a miracle. God had never failed me, and I just knew that He wasn't going to allow my husband to die. He was the only person beside my grandmother and children whom I knew loved me, and once again, just like with my grandmother, I had no time to fully mourn his passing. He was the father of my children. Was I cursed? I had done everything in my power not to be like my mom. How could this be happening to me? If my kids lose their father, they will be fatherless like I was. How could I do it all on my own? I didn't know the answer, but I found myself doing it. God had given me a strength I didn't know I had, and He showed me how to use it.

We never know what life is going to bring, nor are we ever fully prepared for obstacles that may come. Some things will feel unbearable and like they will never end, but stay the course. It's not forever. Many days I wanted to fold but my dreams, and my children kept me standing and pushing on. Everyone tells me how strong I am, and honestly, most times I don't feel strong at all. I just know that I can't give up. I just know that no matter what, I've got to keep going. You may feel weak. You may not have all the answers. But you are going to get you through it. So just keep pushing.

Things Not Seen

SHERRI PICKETT

"Now faith is the substance of things hoped for, the evidence of things not seen." —Hebrews 11:1

My faith is the foundation on which I stand. It doesn't mean that life is easier. It holds me up. Sometimes, it carries me through.

"The ultrasound revealed that you only have two vessels in your umbilical cord. Normally, there should be three. I am referring you to another doctor for a more advanced ultrasound."

I was in shock. I was not sure what this meant. But something was wrong. When I got home, I called my cousin Patricia. I could not speak after I said hello. Tears welled up in my eyes.

"Sherri, is everything okay?"

When I was finally able to get audible words out, I said, "There might be something wrong with the baby."

Unfortunately, she could not understand the words through my blubbering. "What did you say?"

Clearer, I said, "There might be something wrong with the baby." A flood of tears emerged from my eyes.

"Hold on, I'll be right over."

She calmed me down, and I explained the situation. She insisted that I call and make the appointment right away. Two weeks later, I traveled with her and another cousin to Plano, Texas. The 3D image ultrasound confirmed that I only had two vessels. There was a risk that the baby could have a heart defect, kidney problems, or even a genetic abnormality. According to the doctor's assistant, the baby could also be fine. She was the result of a two-vessel pregnancy.

My mind took me down a rabbit hole of negative thoughts. So many things already weighed heavily on my mind. The last six months had been filled with a spiraling tornado of problems.

It all began when my dad was placed on hospice with terminal liver cancer. My mom had Stage IV Alzheimer's. On April 28, I quit my job to care for my parents. My dad died on May 2. I stayed about a week and returned home to my family. About three weeks later, my husband thought it was a good time to serve me with divorce papers. The last 10 years had been rocky, but I always hoped my marriage would work. I was distraught, but I couldn't give those feelings much thought. My main concern was my mom living at home alone. So the day after school let out, I traveled 1500 miles from Barstow, California to Daingerfield, Texas with five children to live in one bedroom to help take care of my mom. My objective was to get her affairs in order to place her into a nursing home. It took much longer than I anticipated. My children had to begin school in Texas in September. Sometimes my mom knew us, and sometimes she didn't.

"I don't know who that heifer is in there!" she exclaimed one day. My mom, believing I was a stranger in her home, took a picture frame and started hitting me with it. The emotional rollercoaster was weighing heavily on me, and I needed help. The facilitator at the Alzheimer's support group advised me to get her into a nursing home quickly. Ultimately, one of us would be there. Either she was going or I was going to lose my mind to the point of needing to go for myself. The plan that was discussed at her doctor's appointment was to get her admitted into the hospital and then transferred to the nursing home. Refusing to be admitted, the plan didn't work, and I was in tears, steaming mad. I went to a nursing home and spoke with the administrator who listened and understood my frustration. I was distraught when I went into her office. She didn't even know my mother was in the parking lot. I had a cousin who worked at that very facility, and the administrator suggested we bring my mother in under the guise of having lunch with my cousin. I completed her paperwork and then went home to get her clothes. This gave me some needed relief.

My husband came to visit us in November. I practically begged him for one last shebang. I later found out that he was hesitant because he had a girlfriend. He cheated on his girlfriend with me, his wife. As if I had not dealt with enough already, I found out I was pregnant with my sixth child, yes, by my soon-to-be-ex-husband. Then being told I only had two vessels instead of three and the problems that could arise with my baby, I thought to myself, "Didn't God know that I had met my quota for problems for that year?" My heart ached, and I cried many tears. My divorce was finalized in December. It took a few more months to get my mom's affairs settled. I decided to move back home to have my baby. In March, my ex-husband helped to move us back to my house.

I knew the potential problems that lied ahead for this pregnancy, so I made my appointments as soon as I moved back. My obstetrician reviewed my records and ordered another ultrasound. "Do you know that you only have two vessels?" the ultrasound technician asked.

"Yes, I know," I said irritated. Between my father passing, my mom not knowing who I was, the divorce, and being overly concerned about my pregnancy, sleep did not come easy. On many occasions, I calmed my nerves by walking through my neighborhood at night. All along the way, I talked to God. Our conversations included the relationship with my ex-husband, finances, and my mother's health. But my primary prayer request was that my baby would be okay.

My doctor scheduled me for non-stress tests once a week, then twice a week. The non-stress tests were stressful. Fear continuously crept in. I began having contractions early. My labor had to be stopped. I inevitably went into labor on May 10, my dad's birthday. This was 21 days before my due date. My baby boy was born at 11:30 a.m. on May 11. He weighed seven pounds and three ounces. After a few minutes of bonding, the nurses took him to be evaluated by the pediatrician. He then came in and informed my ex-husband and me of the results.

"You have a healthy baby boy. Would you like to have him circumcised?"

"Yes." I paused. "He's okay?"

"He's fine."

He walked to the door and opened it. He turned around before he exited and said, "By the way, you had all three vessels."

I could not believe it. The third vessel could not be seen on any of the ultrasounds. It was there the entire time. God seemed to be missing during that challenging year, but He was always there, too.

Three years passed, and my mother's condition progressed. She became bed bound. She could not speak or swallow food. Do not resuscitate forms were faxed to my job. On the night of September 12, I received the phone call. She had passed. My ex-husband was with me and he comforted me. This began a new relationship. A month later, I was pregnant again. I was 38 years old. Everything was going fine with the pregnancy. I was doing exceptionally well at gaining weight. At about 36 weeks, my doctor sent me to a high-risk obstetrician for another ultrasound.

I thought, "Here we go again."

"I don't see anything wrong. Why did your doctor send you here?"

"I don't know. He didn't say."

"Everything looks fine to me."

I was relieved that nothing was wrong. At 38 weeks, my children and I moved into another home to accommodate our new edition. Growing impatient with the birth, I had trouble sleeping during those warm summer nights. Once again, I began my nocturnal walks through the new neighborhood. Streetlights lit my path as I became familiar with the new streets. I casually talked to God like an old friend and expressed my concerns about life. I prayed for others and I was also thankful for answered prayers. I prayed for the baby to arrive healthy.

My due date came and went without a baby. This was the first time that I was overdue. The opportunity for my two older girls to be present during the birth was not an option anymore. The first day of school coincided with being induced at 41 weeks. My ex-husband and I walked three children to the nearby elementary school, and then I went to my doctor's appointment. The doctor discussed the induction and then he examined me. I was five centimeters dilated and I had not felt any contractions. That was different. Normally, I would have been in excruciating pain.

"That's great," the doctor said. "I'm sending you to the hospital right now. They will still give you something to keep you progressing."

I went home and got a few things together, and my ex-husband drove me to the hospital. I continued to contract and progress on my own naturally. The pain was evidence that I was truly in labor. When I was examined again, I was at seven centimeters. But the monitor showed the baby's heart rate dropping with each contraction. My doctor quickly made a decision to do an emergency C-section. I was disappointed. I was familiar with the recovery of a C-section from my first pregnancy. Life was going to be complicated with six children and a newborn.

The culmination of everything caused me to have an out of body experience. I rose to the ceiling and saw myself peacefully lying in the hospital bed. I returned to myself, and the anesthesiologist came in and gave me the epidural before being wheeled into the operating room. A few minutes later, I was pleasantly surprised by "It's a boy!" I did not know the gender beforehand. I was convinced it was a girl. The final score was four girls and three boys. I was immediately getting a tubal ligation. Then I heard whispers from the husband and wife obstetrical team.

"Why didn't we see this before?"

I didn't know what they saw. After I was sent to the recovery room, the doctor came in and said, "Your placenta grew through your uterus. The condition is called placenta percreta. The placenta won't come out. We need to send you to a nearby hospital because this hospital is not equipped to handle this. The ambulance will be ready shortly."

He left the room, and I was confused.

The traveling nurse calmly said, "I had a patient who had that before."

That briefly brought me a sense of relief. I thought it was a common condition.

She continued, "The mother and baby died."

At that moment, I realized how serious my condition was. There are three types of accreta conditions, and placenta percreta is the least common. I was possibly three centimeters from death. If I had delivered naturally, I could have hemorrhaged to death. When the ambulance was ready, I was driven over an hour away to another hospital without my newborn baby. After I was settled into my room, the doctor came in with his team.

"I'm so glad to see you," the doctor greeted me. "It's a miracle that you are here."

He introduced the team that would be assisting him. I was scheduled for an MRI the next day and encouraged to walk around the nurses' station to help recover from the C-section. I slowly paced myself as I took one small step in front of the other. There were positive quotes and scriptures that encouraged me as I passed each door. I paused for a moment.

A nurse asked in a sympathetic voice, "Oh, honey, where's your mother?" My heart sank. I was all alone. I was reminded that the next month was the anniversary of my mother's death. I did not have a mother to help take care of me. As I choked up, I replied, "She's deceased." I walked back to my room and cried.

The following day, the MRI revealed that the placenta had traveled to my bladder. The implications were explained, if the placenta had attached to my bladder, there was a probability that a portion of my bladder would be cut off and I would have to use a Foley catheter for a few weeks. The only remedy to remove the placenta was a partial hysterectomy. My ovaries would remain intact.

I needed to call someone. I could only make local calls from the hospital phone. My cell phone was at home. I had memorized my cousin's phone number.

"You had the baby? Where are you calling from? I am close by. I'll be there after work."

In the meanwhile, the doctor came by to check on me.

"Where is her baby?" the doctor asked.

"At the other hospital," the nurse replied.

"She needs to be with her baby."

The baby would not be a patient at the hospital, but a visitor. He needed someone to be with him the entire time. My cousin and her husband agreed to take shifts and stay at the hospital with the baby. When my newborn baby was released from the hospital, my ex-husband brought him to me. The following day, the surgery was a success. The surgeon was able to peel the placenta off my bladder because it had not yet attached. I lost a lot of blood and received a blood transfusion. Two surgeries within a few days was going to be an ordeal. I tried to bond with my newborn baby the best that I could. We failed at breastfeeding, and he had to be formula fed. My cousins had prior commitments, so a good friend came to stay with me and the baby the last two days. After running a fever, I was finally released after a week. It was a slow recovery, but I healed well. I was even able to breastfeed my baby after meeting with a lactation consultant.

This birth plan was completely orchestrated by God. There were so many behind-the-scenes occurrences. Both of these pregnancies were a testament to my faith. Even though it wasn't easy and I was met with back-to-back emotional obstacles, I was able to persevere through each life-changing event. God sent support when I needed it. He was there even when I thought He wasn't. I am blessed that I had positive outcomes. With everything I've been through, I am always reminded that God's love is with me. Whatever problems that may arise in my life, I have to continue to trust in God, even when things are not seen.

My Black and Blue Angels

SHIRRELL F. EDEY, MBA

My mother named me Shirrell after the 1960s group "The Shirelles" and tweaked the spelling a bit to her liking. I grew to be known as "Pooksie" to my mom and "The Kid" to my dad, but I would have to learn who I was, and I took a long, dark path to get there.

Low self-esteem, lack of self-worth, and substance abuse gave me a one-way ticket to self-destruction. There were times I caught my reflection in a storefront window and didn't recognize who I was. I hated the sun. It was easier to hide in the dark. I didn't want anyone to see "me" or who I had become. Looking back, my childhood was so full of love, fun, family, and friends. No one would have ever predicted I would need to climb out of the dark abyss that was my life. I prayed to God to be rescued before my family received word I was found dead at the hands of another, or even worse, my own hands. Suicide was a thought I had all too often.

Are you familiar with the saying "Be careful what you pray for"? Well, I have a testimony that speaks directly to that advice which will put its true meaning into perspective. God's answers may not arrive in the form you imagine.

I used drugs as often as I could breathe to numb the pain of my past and present trying to run from the psychological and emotional issues when in fact I was on a collision course to them. I ran from place to place, person to person, and into toxic relationships trying to escape the empty shell of myself, but everywhere I went, there I was. "Lord, please help me find my way home! Lord, please rescue me!"

My storm began at the tender age of 13. Growing up, I was smart, beautiful, loving, and caring but completely unaware of these attributes. People saw in me what I failed to see in myself. My body started to develop, getting me the wrong kind of attention. I was young and easily influenced, which in hindsight, completely contradicted the "smart" in me. My desperation for attention, no matter the source, drew me in whatever direction from which the attention was coming. In my case, it was the bad boys and girls in school. I wanted to be popular, to be cool. The strange thing was that I was a homecoming queen and a cheerleader, earned excellent grades, and had a car by the time I was 16 years old. Not someone you'd think needed any additional attention.

Since many of the cool kids were failing school, I injected myself into their lives by offering to help with studying and homework. Once in with the cool crew, I dumbed myself down to blend in. I graduated to following their deviant behavior by ditching school and smoking weed and cigarettes (which made me sick to my stomach), but I had to do it to fit in. My mother caught on *very* quickly and forbade me from hanging with my "friends." In typical teenage fashion, I rebelled. So did my mom.

I thought I was sneaking out of the house one night and heading to a party. I quietly unlocked, opened, and climbed out my bedroom window, which faced the driveway to our beautiful San Fernando Valley home. I closed the window thinking I was on my way. I turned to face the driveway, and my mom was standing there! It wasn't the first time I'd gotten into trouble, but it would be the beginning of a ten-year rollercoaster ride I desperately wanted off of. She told me to pack my things and that she was dropping me off at my father's house—in Compton. Reality check 101! I'd never lived with my father before. It was like I was meeting him for the first time. He was a "cool" dad. But that's not what I needed at 14 years old. I needed a father.

His opening statement? "Hey kid, come on in here. That's your room. I know you smoke weed, and I don't want you doing it out in the streets. The stash box is on my dresser with zig-zags in it. Go on in there and roll a joint so we can get you settled in." I did as I was told. I had no idea I moved into the twilight party zone.

In the 80s, we had one of the few homes in the area with a pool, so our house was the place to be. My dad was a tremendous cook and a BBQ grill master! There were always people coming in and out all times of the day and night drinking, smoking weed, playing dominoes, and doing another drug that had a sweet burning smell. I didn't understand it at the time, but I would sooner than later.

Dad's friends would come home with him from work or arrive shortly after he did almost daily. I was new to the neighborhood and didn't know many kids my age, so I hung around at home being introduced to dad's friends. He never saw the way they looked at me when he wasn't around. The way they brushed against me in passing with a fake "oops." When my father was outside, off with his women, or making a run to the store, that "oops" turned into sneaking in my room to touch and fondle me. I was afraid to tell my dad or anyone else for that matter. But then he became the perpetrator. My silence deepened. He would say, "You know, you look just like your mother." I never understood how he could know that from the darkness of my room he entered at night. From 14 to 17 years old, I "survived" sickening male trespasses by being high out of my mind. I toggled between parents depending on my behavior. By my senior year of high school, I'd landed back at my dad's house. One day, he called me into the kitchen, pulled out a glass pipe filled with cocaine, and said "try this." I knew then what the sweet burning smell was. I was hooked instantly. It was numbness I needed to escape my mind and body, and I left home at 17 to chase that high.

No more emotions, love, friendships, or family. I was done with it all. It made me too human. The high was my refuge. I became a regular in a few of the local dope houses. I was the life of the party. Making people laugh was my sick distraction from looking in the mirror. I believed somehow I was "better" than the addicts around me. I wasn't an addict. I was a social cocaine user who could stop anytime. By 21, I had a nice car, and I even had a husband and a home. I didn't need the drug to survive, because girls just want to have fun, right? Wrong! This girl just wanted to be numb. I was in total denial. Staying high kept me from feeling and quieted my thoughts.

In one of my fogs, I was asked, "What would make you stop using drugs? You are so much smarter than 'this' and truly special. You don't belong here."

I replied, "If I ever got pregnant." Mission accomplished. However, he never planned on being a father.

The pregnancy made me put the drugs down. I vowed to be the best mom. However, the dream was short lived. Becoming a mom was a temporary fix. It couldn't take away the unhealed brokenness so deep in me. Not dealing with my issues landed me back in the streets, and I relapsed just two years after she was born.

Drug addicts usually escalate to criminal activities to support their habit, and I was no different. This caused me to spend short stints in jail. I was living in a category-5 hurricane with no signs of brighter days. During a three-day drug binge, I became sick to my stomach, throwing up violently. I yelled at the zombie in the room to close the curtain, because I could see the sun, which meant the sun could see me. The zombie said, "Let it shine. It's God's work." In that moment, the tears began to silently fall. I had no idea where this was coming from. I didn't feel. How could I? I had been using for three consecutive days with no sleep. And yet I couldn't stop the tears. It felt as if they were cleansing my soul. Prayer leaped from my spirit, and I asked God to take me from this life, this pain, and this insanity. I'm hopeless and helpless against my addiction. Please, Lord, rescue me! Amen. The rescue could have been my life. I just wanted it to end. God had different plans.

I dried my tears and realized I had to get more drugs before sundown. I went into a nearby mall to use some stolen gift cards to purchase some items I could sell to get more drugs. The cashier rang the items up and placed them in a bag, and I was on my merry way. As I exited the store, I was approached by mall security, detained, taken to an office, and informed that they were aware of the gift card fraud. I had been caught red handed. They called LAPD, and I was arrested. Or had I been rescued?

My life had caught up with me. After taking my fingerprints, they found all of the aliases I had used to keep from doing hard time. They combined the previous convictions and charged me with multiple felony counts. I wasn't going home for a while this time. When I was booked into the county jail yet again, I was taken to the jail infirmary because my blood pressure was dangerously low. I was dizzy and vomiting and weighed a mere 101 pounds. After taking urine and blood tests, the nurse asked, "Did you know you were pregnant?" I was devastated. I was two months along.

What was I going to do with another baby? My family had custody of my daughter already, and I couldn't even take care of myself much less a second child. By the time I decided to terminate the pregnancy, I was in my second trimester and had to have a two-day procedure known as a dilation and evacuation (D&E). I was called by the rehab program counselor and told officers were coming to escort me for the procedure. I arrived at the facility and changed clothes and was shackled to a bed and wheeled to an exam room. A doctor came in and explained the procedure, had me sign to consent, and told me to put my legs in the stirrups. He explained I would feel a little pressure with the insertion to start dilation, and the evacuation of the fetus would happen the following day. I gave a nod to acknowledge my understanding. He said, "Okay, here we go." The tears started to flow. I thought of how beautiful my daughter was and how beautiful I know I can be. I looked to God. I sat up quickly and told the doctor to stop. He asked if he hurt me because he hadn't done anything yet. I knew he hadn't, and I didn't want him to. I cried out "I'm gonna keep my baby." He removed his surgical gloves, walked over to his lab coat hanging on a hook, reached in the pocket, and pulled out rosary beads. He laid it on my belly as I sobbed and said, "Thank you for giving this child a chance at life." He began to pray over me and my unborn child.

Today, that child, my son, is a 25-year-old super star who received a full Mechanical Engineering scholarship and aspires to be a day trader. My daughter is a talented vocalist with an established customer service background. My children were born from the worst part of me. They became the best part of me and my strongest why during my recovery. I chose to be open and honest with them about my past. Through my transparency, they were able to forgive me. I will always be grateful for the nonjudgmental love they continuously show me.

Year after year, I struggled with the pain of the drug-induced and perverted delusions that my father had of me being a younger version of my mother. I struggled with the pain of his friends molesting me with their eyes and then their hands and the pain of me believing it was my fault for getting in so much trouble that I was sent to live there. The dark road I took to mask the pain changed the course of my life forever, and the road to better wasn't easy.

The day I cried out to God to save me from substance abuse and self-destruction, I expected him to remove the cocaine from me and return me to a healthy great life. God sent angels unlike anything I could have imagined. When I was arrested at the mall, the officer in blue was the first angel, and he would adorn my wrists with silver bracelets. I had plans on going in and getting right out. The judge, who I had before, recognized me and said, " I told you if I saw you again, you were going to jail." He sentenced me to 16 months in prison. Angry and defiant, I called that judge all kinds of names in my head. During my incarceration, there were no drugs to keep me numb. I would be alone at night with my thoughts and no way to escape them. I was forced to dig to the depths of my core and speak the truth of the things that happened to me, acknowledging a past I desperately had been trying to avoid. I couldn't do anything in prison but heal. I was determined to learn how to love that woman staring at me in the mirror. She was worthy.

That judge, sitting there in his black robe banging his gavel, became my second angel. His sentencing me changed my life. When I finished my sentence, I was clear I was never going back. I knew I could do and be better in life for me and my kids. I continued to do the work to stay off drugs. I went back to school until I got my MBA. I worked in Corporate America for over 30 years before God shifted me into my purpose as an entrepreneur doing what I love—catering and event planning.

I thank God for answering my prayers by sending me my angels in blue and black to save my life. I thank him for exposing me to me. When praying for a way out of anything, know that the answer may not look how you think it should, but if you trust and have faith, it will be revealed. Follow the path God has for you through your healing. It will be worth it, and you are worth it.

Looking for Love in All the Wrong Faces

SHONTA' TAYLOR

Your early years can have a preeminent impact on the course of life you decide to take. My experiences led me on a destructive cycle of looking for love in all the wrong faces. After multiple failed attempts to receive love and give it, I had to accept the painful truth that I didn't know what love was. I sought love through the attention and devotion of men. I felt validated by material possessions and money because my self-worth was determined by what I presented to the world on the outside instead of who I truly was on the inside. I came to a point in my life where I was sick of dysfunction and heartbreak. I was tired of being misused and abused, so I went on a quest in hopes to discover what love is.

My journey began at my great-grandmother's house, where I lived with my little brother, six younger cousins, and five adult cousins. My Ga-Ga was old but strong, wise, resilient, and attentive to the needs of all of us. She did her best to protect and provide for me, however, she didn't have eyes and ears everywhere to shield me from all that I saw, heard, and endured.

I witnessed my cousins physically abuse their women, and I saw the aftermath of my relative savagely beaten and left to walk up the street naked. I often wondered, "Why did this happen?" I was told it was love. It would be explained that they are working things out. I thought to myself, "If this is love, I want no parts of it." The problem was that while I wanted no parts of the love I saw growing up, I never saw what healthy love looked like.

I listened to my Ga-Ga's desperate prayers for God to free her grandchildren from the grips of addiction and to protect us from all hurt, harm, and danger. There were remnants of crack and pipes on floors and dressers. I saw my aunt repeatedly pay off debts to the dope man to keep our family from being harmed. With all that I witnessed, I shouted my Amens as Ga-Ga prayed.

Growing up, I didn't have much. With all the adults in the house suffering from some type of addiction, there was no one to fully provide for me and my younger cousins. Pouring anything positive into us was non-existent. It didn't take long before kids at school started bullying and teasing me for my outdated clothes, which were, of course, hand-me-downs or thrift store bought, and nothing ever had a label on it. I was constantly picked on and had to fight without the skills to do so. As a result, I became fearful and insecure about my self-image.

I secretly started hanging out with a girl named Angel who was a few years older than me. She could fight. Around her, no one bothered me. I also admired her nice clothes and name brands, and she always had money—something I didn't have. Angel took me under her wing, and I was honored she befriended a scrub like me. She taught me how to shoplift the things I wanted. I knew it was wrong, but I looked up to her and wanted to be just like her. I revered our friendship, and I thought nobody could ever come between us. When Angel met an older dude, she dropped me like a bad habit. I felt betrayed, confused, and worthless. She didn't value me the way I valued her.

While working at a Summer Youth Work Program, I met a group of teen girls. They all had gangsta boyfriends dropping them off and picking them up from work while I was standing in the hot sun sweating at the bus stop. I wanted a handsome hunk of a thug in my life too, and to my surprise, I had an older guy checking me out the whole time.

Donovan, a known gang banger and drug dealer five years my senior, was interested in me. At 13 years old, having an older guy interested in me made me feel special. One day, Donovan, who I nicknamed Don, showed up at my job with lunch from a local burger stand. He handed me my food and wrote his pager number on the container filled with chili cheese fries. His note on the box said "Beep me when you get off work." I stood there frozen like a deer in headlights, but I fought through my nerves and mumbled, "Okay." Once he left the office, my co-workers and I screamed and celebrated like little school girls do when they see their crush. I was excited but overwhelmed. I had never dated before. I didn't understand the emotional dynamics of a young pubescent adolescent girl losing her sanity after having her first ride on the male's joystick, but at 13, dating an older man, I would eventually find out.

Don swept me off my feet by spoiling me. Looking back, it's easy to sweep someone off their feet who's never had much. He got my nails done every two weeks, took me shopping for school clothes every year, and bought me Turkish link chains and bamboo earrings—but not two pairs. I went from being bullied and teased to being nicknamed Hollywood and welcomed into all the popular circles at my high school. I joked around declaring that Don was my "Captain Save a Hoe" because I needed saving. I now realize I didn't need the type of saving he provided.

I sneaked around to see him as much as I could, even lying to my mom about babysitting just to go on dates with him. He had become cocaine, and I was the dope fiend always looking for my next hit of him. I was meeting up with him at sleazy motels or hanging out at the dope house. I wasn't worried about the danger I was putting myself in. When I was with Don, nothing else mattered.

Although I felt remorse for my poor choices, it didn't stop me. My relationship with him consumed every waking moment of my life. I couldn't focus on classwork when I actually went to class. I had arguments and fist fights with older girls with whom he was cheating. I used to hide his drugs in my private feminine area when the police pulled us over, not taking into account that if the police had searched me, I would've been locked up! I was proud to be the Bonnie to his Clyde, but then came the straw that broke the camel's back.

One night while hanging out at Don's friend's house, we got into a heated discussion about a lady who kept paging him. I demanded to be taken home. Don loaned his car out to one of his errand boys. Tired of hearing us argue, his friend Jooney threw him the keys to his car to take me home. My mom's house was enemy territory for Don. Usually he would drop me off at the corner store, but for some reason unknown to me, he pulled right up in my mom's driveway.

I thought it was odd considering his enemies were hanging out directly across the street. I didn't say anything because I figured he was strapped. We sat in the car with the windows down while he apologized for his cheating. Out of nowhere, a masked gunman ran up to the driver's side window and put a gun against Don's head. The gunman aggressively yelled at me to get out of the car or he'd blow Don's head off. I was frantically crying, "No, please! No!" while getting out of the car at the same time. The gunman ordered Don out of the car, and he jumped in and drove off. We ran into my house and called Jooney. Next thing I knew, three car loads of thugs pulled up ready to kill anything that moved, but it was a ghost town on my block after the carjacking occurred. A few days passed, and Jooney's car was found stripped and set on fire. Don made compensation arrangements with Jooney for the car, so I assumed everything was fine, but it wasn't.

Jooney thought I had Don set up and jacked for the car. I tried to explain that I would never do that, but his mind was made up that I did. He knocked me out in the middle of the street. When I woke up, I saw my cousin on top of his head hitting him with a mini hammer she always carried in her purse. I'm so grateful she was there because I don't know what his intentions were. I called Don to tell him what happened, and he did nothing to defend me. This infuriated me, so I broke up with him. Once again, just like with Angel, I felt worthless. A few years went by, and we occasionally messed around, but it was never the same. Now being an adult, I didn't want that thug life anymore. Don ended up dying in a terrible car accident, and I continued to look for love in all the wrong faces.

You would think I would've learned my lesson after having such a tumultuous relationship with a gangsta drug dealer, but I didn't. I fell head over heels for a bank robber, next a pimp, and then I ended the cycle of dysfunctional dating by marrying a male exotic dancer. I was chasing the high I got when I was with Don. What a man would buy and provide, I equated to love, and the highest bidder won. It didn't matter what I had to suffer. I was determined never to be the poor broke girl who was bullied and laughed at again. When the marriage fell apart, I stopped looking for love because it was evident I had no clue what it was, looked like, or felt like. I couldn't find something I'd never had. I thought I needed someone to fill the void I felt in my spirit not realizing that my spirit is a divine entity, therefore it yearns for something bigger than my carnal mind could fathom. I suffered the mental angst of wanting healing and missing the hustle of the fast life. It was a constant tug of war, but only one would win.

One night, pain gripped my heart so tight, I thought I was having a heart attack. It was an emotional breakdown. All the hurt, lies, betrayals, and violence had taken a toll on me. I was hyperventilating as the movie of my life and every negative choice I made played in my mind.

I sat on the edge of my bed gasping for air with tears rolling down my cheeks. I knew I couldn't keep living like this. I opened my mouth and said, "God, help me!" I wasn't even sure God knew who I was. To my surprise, God reminded me through divine recollection of a scripture my godfather often quoted: "Seek ye first the kingdom of God, and his righteousness; and all these things shall be added unto you" (Matthew 6:33). For the first time in my life, scripture became my cardiopulmonary resuscitation, and I began to breathe at a steady pace. It was as if the very breath of God was breathing for me. I never thought to seek the spirit of God, who is the essence of love. In my lowest moments, there He was comforting me and guiding me through as He had been trying to do, but I wasn't aware of it. When Angel dropped me like a bad habit, God was trying to get my attention. When I was carjacked at gunpoint, God was trying to get my attention. God is love, and He was there all along, but because I had no clue what love was, I certainly couldn't recognize the love God was continuously trying to show me.

When God spoke to me, the worthless, loveless, broken woman whom I thought He didn't know, I vowed to build my relationship with Him. I was desperate for a change. After chasing all the wrong things to fill my spirit, I now wanted to be filled with His grace. I knew God would never make me feel like I did in those relationships I once idolized.

I read the Bible daily. God was showing me how to deconstruct every negative thought I had about myself. Every lie I believed as a child was counteracted by the truth in God's word. I read, "I will praise thee; for I am fearfully and wonderfully made" (Psalm 139:14) and "[Nothing] shall be able to separate us from the love of God" (Romans 8:38). I acknowledged this truth and understood that surviving wasn't good enough, but thriving became my goal. I began to fill every distressed portion of my life with the fruits of God's spirit—peace, joy, self-control, patience, kindness, goodness, faithfulness, gentleness, and love.

Going back to that wild life was never an option for me, and that was a promise to myself and God. I broke off every relationship that didn't contribute to me becoming whole and chose to practice celibacy. I wanted to live the life God had for me, and I began to follow his orders. When he put something in my spirit, I did it. I practiced truth telling and prayer. I went back to school to get my high school diploma. I completed Bible school. I became a missionary and then Evangelist. It was important to me to share God's greatness over my life by sharing my personal testimony. His love brought harmony to the chaos I had lived.

The most powerful love God showed me was the respect and love of my children. They look at me and tell me how proud they are. My relationship with them has grown from one of only being a provider who bought them things to make up for not being emotionally available to being an example to whom they could look up. In my spiritual awakening, I learned how to love them and became their mom.

The more I committed myself to God and his righteousness, the more his love illuminated in and through me. When I look at myself in the mirror, I no longer see the face of a broken woman. I see the reflection of love looking at me. The irony of this story is that I was looking for love in all the wrong faces, but love revealed the face I needed to seek. Now that I've found love, I can never lose it, because it lives in me. I'm so grateful for God's unconditional love. In my life, it has been the greatest love of all.

Permission to Be Fearless

TASHA CHAMPION

As children, we look at adults like, "Wow! They go where they want, they do what they want, and they live how they choose," and we think it will be that simple when we become the adult. For many years, I wasn't privy to the struggles adults had, or maybe I was simply being a child and not paying attention. You never think as a kid that life would present obstacles to impede on any part of your dreams. The fairytale of life was nothing more than just a princess ready to be kissed by a prince for life to be magical. Yes, I really thought this was the reality you live in when you become an adult.

Throughout my childhood and teen years, I wasn't supported in things I wanted to do, like act, sing, and dance—pretty much whatever got me in front of a camera because I wasn't shy. I began to believe the lack of support must mean a lack of talent. Support and encouragement start in the home, and I did not have them there. Some things I figured out on my own. I would go on to work with one of the biggest legends in hip hop and come very close to a record deal. Looking back, I wonder if the doubts of success played a part in that falling through. I would think, "What if we [my group] flop? What if we make it big and then can't deliver anymore?" I had no idea this was considered fear. I assumed that these were normal questions, and yes, they were, but when you never move past the what ifs, the fear has taken over.

Ten days after turning 19, I found out I was pregnant with my daughter. I had only been with her father for three months. Although, I was living on my own and working, I was still a statistic. Oftentimes, I thought about being an unmarried teenage mom. Her father assured me he would be there, so in my mind, I was the special statistic who wasn't like the other girls. Our relationship would go on to be a tumultuous one, off and on for 13 years. This would include three more kids and a marriage that never should have happened.

I spent a good portion of my adult life with him. To be honest, marrying him came from a lot of fear as well. Before we got married, we had three kids. Would someone want to be with and marry me with three children? When he asked, it felt like the safe thing to do. I wouldn't have to worry about being a single mom wanting a marriage. Well, I ended up being a single mom inside my marriage. The time I could have been discovering myself, I was being a mom and a wife, putting my hopes and dreams on the back burner. I thought as a mom, my kids came first. Was I really putting my hopes and dreams on pause, or was that the excuse to mask the fear of ever being more than I thought I was? I wanted to apply for jobs for which I knew I qualified, but if they were offering "too much" money, I wouldn't apply. Who was going to actually pay me that salary? Who was I to ask for that amount? The undervalued self talk was real, and I talked myself out of some of the best situations in which I could've put myself. I spent a lot of time in the clouds thinking about things I wanted to do, such as start a day care, start a non-profit for families who don't qualify for public assistance and live just under middle class, and go back to school. The minute I would start to work on any of these things, one question would pop into my mind: "Can you really do this?" Believe it or not, that would shut me down. If I talked to anyone about my dreams, all it took was one comment I deemed as negative, and their thought became my truth. I suffered in silence knowing I could give up before I got started. I was stuck in fear with no clue how to come out of it.

I spent years in my unhappy marriage, being a mom with bad credit, and irresponsible with money management while doing and accepting the bare minimum. I felt unproductive and uninspired. I secretly longed to be others around me who had more, but my default was rich heart, broke mindset. My heart was full of things I wanted, but my mindset wasn't attached. I wanted more for me and my kids, but I was stuck in a mental wheelchair, paralyzed by fear, afraid to take a chance, be told no, or tell anyone how I felt. At some point, I accepted this as my life, my reality, believing this is just the way it is.

I'm sure everyone understands the life you dream of is not always the one you get or that the path to get there has more storms and roadblocks than expected. Sometimes you realize you haven't learned or been equipped with the tools to deal with it and being too afraid to ask for help prolongs the ability to move through it. I had a specific way of asking for things. I hinted around, tried to get people to feel sorry for me so they would just offer. This would take having to ask off the table. The embarrassment of my life was literally holding me hostage. Asking for help would mean admitting there was a problem. It would be letting people know I was an adult and a mom but couldn't figure out so much of my life or how to get it in order. Imagine for a moment never having enough money, not being able to move into a bigger place for your family, always having limits, and providing for your children with that limited mindset. None of this is what my children deserved, and guilt often set in as I looked at them. Their innocent little faces and spirits would one day come to know that mommy didn't do enough, and because of that, they suffered. How could they forgive me if I didn't change? I often wondered if my kids would grow to be ashamed of me because we did not have the big house or a new car. They didn't have their own rooms. Hell, oftentimes I had no furniture and we slept on the floor. I kept saying it would get better, and as a mom, they believed me, but it never changed, and I assumed one day they would see me as a liar. I prayed for a change, but was I actually listening to the answers?

One day, a friend called and said I was on her spirit to pray for. She asked God to silence all voices around me that were not His. I immediately knew what that meant and began to pray the same prayer over my life. What I didn't know was the voices that needed to be silenced were the ones in my own head. The voices that kept me in fear and doubt.

This part of my life became a vicious cycle, and it got worse. Getting better did not seem to be in my near future. I ended up in a divorce, no surprise there. My "wasband" told me and our children that he needed to restart his life as if he was never married or had children. Before I could even process that, I had entered into a relationship with a woman. We thought we had something special. Jumping into a relationship with all the mental and emotional displacement I was dealing with was not the brightest idea, but it felt safe. Through her verbally abusive behavior and treating me and my children like we were less than, I continued to try and hold on to her. Just like with my ex-husband, I had fears of being alone and someone not seeing I was worth being with. Internally, I felt they just might see what I saw in myself—a single mom of four with no clue what her future would be. I was scared, but I also despised how I felt. I was allowing my children to watch someone be completely disrespectful to us, and I had zero defense.

My wakeup call came when she was upset that I didn't make dinner. The next morning, she took her vehicle and house keys from me. I had to go to work and my kids to school. Fortunately, it was the same place. Being in a small town, it was too early to call for a taxi. We kept walking until one opened. As we walked, she drove right by us playing her gospel music. She intended for us to see her in a car. In her mind, she was teaching me a lesson. After work, we sat outside until she got home to let us in. This is what my life had come to, and I allowed my children to be the casualties. I needed a change. Changing couldn't be more fearful or painful than staying here. The most important thing was that I couldn't stay in this space spiritually, emotionally, or mentally. Yes, I needed to leave physically, and eventually, I did, but if I didn't make changes from the inside out first, I was going to repeat these same habits.

I began working with a life coach, and this was life changing. My spiritual awakening was intense. I released self judgment and went deeper into healing. I craved change, and I was on a level of experiencing it. My first phase was learning and accepting who I was. I was enough, and I deserved to value myself where I was in life. The biggest struggle during this time was acknowledging I played a part in where my life was. Owning the truth of that reality through millions of tears running down my face was a game changer. I couldn't believe I had been living in so much fear, and most of it was fearing the unknown. I was minimizing my growth by not diving into the unknown, never learning what was possible. The healing I experienced became instrumental in the cancer diagnosis I had a year later. I was seeing and feeling life so differently than ever before. Was this an overnight change? Absolutely not. It was and is continuous. There are triggers that can take you back, and I make a choice to never feel like I did all those years. In my fear, I used to forget everything and run. Now I choose to work on myself daily, fighting to face everything and rise, making bold decisions to elevate my life, giving me and my children the life we deserve. I had only dreamed about that, and now I could make it my reality. I learned and implemented manifesting what

I wanted. I included my children in the manifestation so we could all vibrate on the same frequency and call more abundance into our life. I realized I was taking action against the fear and staring it dead in the face.

There came a time when I had to make a decision to be full time in my coaching work and make my own dreams come true or continue to work for someone else and enhance their dreams. I kept giving myself a goal date to end the office life for good. That day came and went so many times. I made up excuses, and really, I was comfortable with the minimum pay I was getting because I was afraid to step out on faith and squash my fears. More income and waking up every day to do what I wanted was on the other side of my fear. As I became fearless, I knew taking this step would be the ultimate test. I walked into my office and gave notice. Best decision ever. My dreams became more alive that day. I wanted to wake up and coach women into their best life, and now I was doing it.

No matter how much of my life I worked on getting together, my issue and unhealthy relationship with money was still plaguing me. I gave myself excuses as to why I had not conquered my fears of money management. I had always been bad and irresponsible with it, and once again I accepted that this was my life. I was uncomfortable talking about money around people. I had nothing to add to those conversations. I loathed seeing people pay for things with cards other than their bank card or buying more than their essentials. "I'm never going to have credit cards or more money for other things" is what I would tell myself. I wanted, actually needed, someone to blame so I could feel better. The only one to blame was the woman in the mirror.

During one of my workshops, my aunt, who was a guest speaker, spoke about not letting her ex-husband dictate what she would be able to do financially for her and her girls. She said women must make their finances a priority—something I had never done. My first thought was, Well she makes enough, and she only had two kids and not four" but the actual truth was that the way I handled money was not good, responsible, or healthy. When she spoke about money with ease, something I was uncomfortable with, it touched my spirit, and that was the financial wakeup call I needed. I thought only financially wealthy people spoke about money with ease. I began getting my finances in order. The first step was to acknowledge where I was in my financial life, and it wasn't pretty. Second, I had to stop telling myself I was bad with money and holding it as truth. Third, because of all the things I had learned, I asked the right people questions and without any embarrassment. Voila! People were open to help, judgment free. I recognized patterns I had and changed them little by little. Changing my perception and relationship with money freed the fear money had over me. I began to see money as an abundance of energy used to support the needs and wants in my life. This was crazy. I never thought I would be the one who saw money in this way. Being financially fit was the final key for me to live fearlessly.

Being fearless doesn't mean you're not afraid. It means the fear will no longer immobilize your ability to move forward. It's about taking action, imperfect action, in spite of the fear. You learn failure exposes what doesn't work and gives you another chance to figure out what does. The only way to succumb to your fear is to allow it to stop you.

My fearless stride in life opened my eyes to clearly see my dreams. Where I once felt life was happening to me, I learned life is happening for me. The good, bad, beautiful, ugly—it all happens for my greater good. I sometimes travel down memory lane thinking, "Wow, it took me this long to get here and experience life like this." I want to say shame on me, but my storms were part of my journey. I often worried about what my actions were teaching my kids. I'm grateful that my daughter saw my actions and decided her life didn't have to be the same. She stepped out into the world with a fearless mindset. I'm also grateful my three sons understand where I was and honor me for where I am now. They, too, see the difference.

I gave myself permission to be the fearless woman I am today, and I urge you to do the same. You deserve it. It can be scary because fear has been part of your comfort. Ask yourself, is this the life I want or deserve? If not, step out on strong faith, and it will push you past your fear. When you learn there's nothing holding you back except you, it changes how you see things and changes how you proceed in life. I used to keep myself down, accepting the defeat of never living out my dreams or having more. Now, I soar to new heights through faith, without limits, conquering the world on my terms, my way—fearlessly!

The Girl with the Star over Her Head

THERESA D. POLLEY-SHELLCROFT, MA, FINE ARTS

*I was born with a star over my head. That star
is the passion for creative expression
as a visual artist.*

My passion is creative expression through the visual arts. This has been my passion since age four. I am now 75. I often wondered if my passion was the correct one or if it was only a "dream." That passion was recently reconfirmed when I opened an art education professional journal and felt a deep twinge and recognition in my spirit. (I am learning to listen to my intuition.) I know the mission of my life is to create and to be a beacon of light to other women, especially African American females. I want to inspire them to follow their dream, especially in the arts, where we have been locked out for so long.

In this world, in this community and society, it is not easy for a female artist of any ethnic background to be taken seriously. We are often treated as though our dream is just that—only a dream, not to be actualized. We as women are not considered as important as male artists. As a college-level art history instructor, I see the scarcity of women artists in textbooks. We are few and far in between, oftentimes stuck in the chapter at the end. Most of the serious study and attention in the world of art is showered upon male artists who are given the freedom to be by society.

When receiving this message of rejection and invisibility from the world, time after time, the negative image becomes internalized, making it hard to hold onto that self-image as a serious artist. As an African American female artist, the vision becomes less and less likely to be realized. Thus, the limitations and challenges become internal and external as we struggle with personal desire and the opportunity to be an artist against this closed door of invisibility.

These are what I have found to be issues, which can become limitations or road blocks if you let them:

1. Self-Doubt: When there is not support and encouragement, we begin to doubt our dreams and passions. This negative feedback comes from the wider world and often from the more familiar world of home, friends, and educational establishments. The thought then is "Maybe this is not the path that I should walk," which becomes the internal conversation. This conflict interferes with full creative expression.

2. Racial Issues: For too long, the African American has not been considered to be capable of the production of fine artworks. This is especially true for African American women. Our art is often taken as a hobby. Educators and gallery owners treat us

in such a passive manner—that is, they pass right over us. Some galleries only consider you worthy if your work looks like current trends in the art world, not your individual expression. Your artistic expression, the extension of who you are, is not validated or encouraged. If your work employs current trends in technique, you are not considered as innovative enough for recognition or inclusion. One gallery owner looked at one of my paintings, and said "Picasso," dismissing my message and my art. In other words, I was imitating Picasso. (Correction: Picasso imitated African art.)

Another critic said it does not look like the art of so and so (any recognized artist). Criticism becomes a two-edged sword—to imitate or not? For me, the most important part of the artwork is the message and the content, not the technique.

3. Invisibility and Ethnic Identity: As an African American female, society has images of me that I am to fit, as if into a box or a cage. These images are not what I have envisioned for myself. As an artist, the world message is that I am to be without ethnic identity—only identifying *as an artist*. If my art reflects my life experiences, then how do I leave my ethnicity or gender out of the equation? Out of the expressive content?

If I separate my ethnicity and experiences from my art, I become two or more persons not fully integrated. In other words, I am to deny who and what I am in order to be accepted as an artist.

4. Resistance: To be an African American female artist is an act of resistance. As the world attempts to prescribe or describe who and what I am to be, how I should behave, and what my roles are, these categories do not include being taken seriously as an artist. If I am not taken seriously, I further doubt my passion and dream. Being a female artist, our work is often compared to and judged against other female artists, as though there is only one way to think, to act, and to create. This comparison and dejection adds to that internal battle of "to be or not to be." I felt caught between being myself or being what someone else wants me to be. In other words, "Stay in my place. Do as I say." Yet, I continue to make art. Standing firm in my art-making is an act of resistance against what society wants me to be and do. Because I was born with a star over my head.

5. Time and Opportunity: As an artist, time and space are required. These are not always provided to us as we go about our daily responsibilities such as employment, family, and children. Time is needed to create, and space is needed to produce. After teaching all day, I found, there is little time or energy to devote to my own personal art. When my son was three, I took my easel and canvas out to paint. My son remarked with surprise,

"Mommy where did that come from?" I realized that my son did not know my passion. I did not demonstrate for him how to follow your star. I was not being who I am with him or with myself. (That has changed. My art is everywhere in the space where I live.)

6. Art is a jealous lover: One of my college painting instructors said to our class that art is a jealous lover, and it is. You often need seclusion and less social interaction to create. There are things that must be left behind for a while. This can be perceived by others as a negative. They do not understand that personal passion and the need for seclusion or sacrifice as paramount to art production.

When a man focuses on his passion or art, we applaud that dedication. As a woman, I am not often afforded that same consideration by society.

BACKGROUND AND FOUNDATION

I was raised in the era of Jim Crow. Full, so-called racial integration was not set forth by law until I was well into college. I grew up in an African American community with love and support. I was never told by family, my teachers, or my community, that I could not be anything I wanted to become. Entering into the outer world of limitation and segregation was a shock. This impacted how I saw myself, and I began to doubt that vision and passion.

I began drawing at the age of four. There were no art books in my home. Yet I had a passion and vision for expressing through art. My family supplied me with materials along with time and space to create. My early educational experiences encouraged my artist drive. Our teachers and parents provided those opportunities for us by establishing Saturday art programs. When facing the limitations of the world, it was this community background and foundation that gave me roots and the power to stand my ground. In addition to drawing and painting, I had dance lessons, piano, flute, guitar, and sewing. My family was firmly behind my artistic development. All of this was supported by the African American Community where I was privileged to have as my village. With this positive foundation of family and community, I developed the love and desire to pass it along to others through community engagement. I understood and understand the power of the arts, music, dance, theater, spoken word, writing, photography, film, and visual arts.

SOLUTION

How have I survived as an African American female artist? What about getting over the hurdles? My foundation of early support is the secret ingredient. These are the lessons that I have learned from this inner/outer struggle.

1. Hold On and Keep the Faith: No matter what the world says, you have to keep that star overhead as your light and guide.

   You must walk the path that you deem your destiny. Follow your passion and block out the naysayers. Surround yourself with like-minded persons on your path.

There is rejection in life, but you cannot let that rejection define who you are and what you will do. I often say when told no, "Watch me!"

I have often questioned myself and come to the same conclusion. If no one saw my art, I would still create. I was born with a star over my head.

2. Honor Your Passion by Carving out Time and Space for Your Creativity: A sacred creative space is essential. For several years, I rented studio space away from my home, which gave me a place to focus on and be with my art. The studio gave me a place to show my art and to offer workshops. I also became a teacher to further enhance and support my love of the arts. Don't let anyone or anything stop you. Follow your artistic heart.

3. Accept Who You Are: We are individuals with our own uniqueness and with our own ways of expression. Accept and develop your vision, your ideas, and your way of expressing it. Resist the temptation to follow in the footsteps of another because others want you to do so. Honor yourself first. As I have often stated in mentoring my son, as well as others and new teachers, "Let no one steal your crown." Be honest with yourself. Be who you are without guilt. Love yourself. When you are true to who you are, others are free to be who they are.

4. Nurture Your Creative Passion: Creative expression requires reflection, meditation, and occasional withdrawal from the world. How can you hear your thoughts and develop your unique voice without reflection and seclusion? These activities are an essential part of the creative process. Honor this process and honor your voice.

   As a graduate student in painting, my days were complete as I arrived in the painting studio at 9 a.m. and stayed until 6 p.m. I was full and fulfilled. Later, when I rented space, I could go there after teaching all day and have space to be me, to be free. Giving yourself this time and space is nurturing your creative passion.

5. Hold on to Your Victories: Each victory is a step forward and a validation. Follow that star. Every venture will not be as successful as you envision, but each venture offers a new lesson to grow and to build.

I often recall the first juried art exhibition I entered. My painting was accepted. I was nineteen years of age. The exhibition included well established artists within a 200-mile radius of the art gallery and museum. When I get discouraged, I reflect back to that time and event. I have had many acceptances and rejections since that time. But that victory and each one since keeps me going because someone is listening, watching, and acknowledging me as an artist.

Many of my art pieces tell the stories and memories in my heart. It has given me freedom and has gotten me through many emotions and trying times. I have learned so much about myself through the growth of my artistic personality and the many challenges I faced being an African American female artist. I continue to allow my love of creative expression to be the driving force against any rejection, naysayers, and even my own self-doubt. Art is the beauty of my spirit on canvas.

CONCLUSION

Have I fully arrived at the age of 75? The answer is no. Life evolves and unfolds in time and over time. Each day, I build on the day before. As a breast cancer survivor, the first thing I learned was to always look for the silver lining. Through every obstacle, choose to find something good to help you endure. With each work of art, whether the content is personal or social commentary, I get to learn more about who I am. As questions are raised through my art, I am challenged to dig deeper and create more. Trust me: I have just begun to climb.

I was born with a star over my head,
As were you!
Follow that star.

Overcoming Trauma: Lessons Learned

danyelle s. goitia beal, MA, BCBA

I was born to a young girl. I was born in jail.

My mother, at nineteen, was awaiting sentencing for the murder of my father: a crime to which she'd admit guilt.

Eventually released, the courts determined that her act of murder was in fact an act of self-defense. She attempted to protect me by giving me her last name for fear of harm to herself and to me. She began a journey of single motherhood. This is how I came into the world. Seemingly, this was my fate.

LIFE IS DIFFICULT

A year and a half after I was born, my mother, gloria, gave birth to my little sister, a product of rape. Years later, she married a man, and together they produced a son. These are my biological siblings. We are all Black. My mother was of Spanish/Mexican cultures. Our skin color was a disgrace to her family, and it was a message that echoed my entire life.

One of the first lessons that I ingested as a young girl was that I was not valued. I understood this through gloria's choices and the myriad of ways I was exposed to pain, trauma, and abuse. My mother's husband had grown sons. This man and one of his sons abused me for years. Because of this, my little sister and I were placed into foster care. We were mostly separated, and for me, additional abuse continued in some of these placements. When we finally returned home, gloria was pregnant with my little brother. I had to continue to live with the man who took away my childhood and my innocence, where the abuse continued until my stepfather suffered a traumatic brain injury in a car accident.

I watched gloria struggle with depression and substance abuse until she died. She recovered from heroin use but continued to battle alcoholism. I witnessed her gradual decline over the formative years of my life. I was angry with her for most of my life and resented her for taking away my paternal family who seemingly wanted me. I was infuriated with her because of her struggle with addiction. She did not protect me, and she chose drugs, alcohol, and men over me. Every time. I was responsible for my siblings, and I was livid about it. This forced responsibility ignited rage towards gloria, my stepfather, and adults. Who was responsible for me? They did not hear my cries; they did not listen to my words, and they did not hear my heart.

LOVE IS POWERFUL

A change occurred in my life with a geographical shift. Our family moved to Victorville, California. I remember periodically driving out to the desert to see progress on a house, and then we were there. I started a new school as a sixth grader: awkward, lanky, clumsy, and attention-seeking, yet apprehensive. I navigated my way through that year and moved onto junior high school. I remember struggling in school and being teased for being different.

That year, I was assigned a teacher named Ms. Long. She was kind and supportive. She was tall, had dark mocha skin and long black hair, and was always patient with me. Ms. Long invited me to participate in a Black History Month event where I was selected to recite Maya Angelou's *Phenomenal Woman*. She told me that I was beautiful despite being told that I was not my whole life. She told me that I was beautiful because of my Blackness not because I was mixed. It was the first time that I remember being seen, and it was the beginning of me learning how to find my heart, my voice, and myself. Ms. Long was the first strong Black woman that I remember making a difference in my life. It shifted my self-perception. I was learning how to love myself.

In high school, I struggled to find myself. Being in a home where I had only heard negative words regarding Black people, specifically Black men, I felt like I had to justify my "Blackness." I had to fight to be me. I experimented with different groups of people and identities. It came out in my behavior throughout my adolescence. Eventually, I established close friendships. These friends took me in during gloria's drunken rages when I felt lost and when I needed love. Their parents fed me, gave me clothes, and mediated arguments that came up between us.

One friend's mother took me in during my eleventh grade year and held on to me so tight. She is still holding on to me and my daughters. One of the first questions she asked upon meeting me was "Where are you going to college?" I had never even thought about it. I assumed that I would take care of my mother and siblings. She literally filled out applications for me, paid the fees, bought me a luggage set, and sent me on my way. She taught me about Toni Morrison and HBCUs. She was strong and caring and provided a framework for motherhood in a way that I had never experienced. Because of her and my friends' mothers, I was able to spread my wings for the first time. I was learning how to be loved.

YOU CAN CHANGE

My first year in college, I found myself pregnant with my daughter. I was living in the dorms. Eventually, I moved in with her father for a short time before and after she was born. One night, he and I got into a huge fight, and I was kicked out of the apartment we shared. I lived in a car with my six-week-old baby girl until a friend reached out to me, learned of my circumstance, and invited me to live with her and her mother until I could get on my feet. I lived with them for some time. I was enthralled to witness a Black single mother and her incredibly beautiful and outspoken daughter. I saw their relationship ebb and flow. I saw them love each other and be a team. My friend's mother cooked the most amazing meals for us. She would also spend her last bit of money to treat us to nice dinners at fancy restaurants. We got dressed, went out, ordered drinks, and ate oysters. I had never experienced this before. There wasn't some fancy occasion, it was just an opportunity for her to share a meal with us because she wanted to. My friend and her mother were surrounded by good friends and laughter and pure joy. She showed me how to experience life, eat delicious food, see the beauty around me, and to enjoy others' company. I watched these beautiful Black women laugh, love, and be wholly honest with each other. It was the first time I had seen the beauty in such a relationship.

I felt another shift; I knew I wanted a different life than I had experienced. I wanted to have the kind of relationship with my own daughter that my friend had with her mother. In witnessing their relationship, I was learning self-care and I was learning how to be a mother.

HEARTBREAK CHANGES YOU

My mother died early in my college journey. She had a stroke that was complicated by liver issues and years of substance abuse. I received 46 calls one night after a long day at school. I needed to rush home because gloria was not going to make it through the night. By the time that I got there, her doctor ushered me into a room and told me that I needed to make a critical decision: life support or she dies. She was completely brain dead with no hope of recovery. Devastation. How? I had just seen her. Two nights before, I'd sent her, my sister, and my newborn nephew home. I had plans, and they showed up unannounced. I was so cruel. I never got to say I was sorry. I kept meaning to call her over the weekend. Now, we were here, and she was brain dead. My mom. gloria. How would I pick up these pieces? I was learning to grieve.

Sometime later, I attended a funeral for my daughter's godfather, who passed from cancer at age 19. Here, the pastor of the church made a call for salvation. I accepted the call and recited Romans 10:9-10. I immediately began attending that church. One Sunday, after I missed three church services while taking care of the memorial arrangements for gloria, a pastor approached me and told me that they missed me. I was shocked. I had not made friends with anyone there and could not understand how he knew that I had not been there for three weeks. When I told him what happened, he prayed with me and told me that the church was there to help. Within the week, he, the senior pastor and some women of the church came to my tiny apartment to bring my family food and money to help with the new expenses I had incurred with the adoption of my then 11-year-old brother. They prayed with me and my household. This simple act of kindness showed me that strangers could love me and my children. That was not the first time that this particular church guided me through life's difficulties. That pastor, his wife, and the congregation are still guiding me and my family through life's shifting tides. Having a spiritual relationship with God and having faith in Him has allowed me to trust that all things can be managed *not* by my own doing but by trusting in God. Through the example of my church, I was learning to give.

RECOVERY IS LONG AND HEALING IS PAINFUL

The first time that I saw a therapist was after gloria died. I was going through a tremendous amount of grief. I thought therapy was for "crazy" people. "I am not crazy, just a bit sad," I thought. I went to see Dr. Paula through my college's mental health services. She helped me work through my immediate loss so that I could deal with my children and complete that year in school.

The second time that I saw a therapist was after a particularly difficult break up with my now husband. Dr. Sarah helped me cope with the heartache I experienced. She was kind and offered an ear. I cried so much in her sessions. She allowed me to pour out my heart without judgment.

The third time that I sought treatment was during an emotional breakdown. I was triggered by a family that I was serving. A mother was addicted to heroin and lost her children to the foster care system. It sent me into a spiral. My boyfriend and I broke up for what I thought was the last time. I lost our home and quit my job. Dr. Nina showed me the truth about my life, my past and present trauma, and my mental health status and provided solutions to actually begin healing. These sessions culminated all of my experiences toward a ladder that I had been avoiding my whole life. I realized that I was angry at my lost childhood, my lost mother, and a life that I could have had. Dr. Nina showed me that I needed to relinquish that anger to be free. A year later, my boyfriend proposed to me, and after experiencing a temporary emotional setback, he said these words to me, "I can't climb down in that hole with you, danyelle. You have to climb up for yourself. This is *your* work. I will be here when you are ready." These words and the work I was doing in therapy helped me understand that for the rest of my life, I alone would have to do the relentlessly difficult work to heal.

Therapy not only allows me to work through the grit and grime that comes up, but to relish the beauty of life. It helps me identify love expressed to me and it gives me permission to love. This is where I learn practical skills for application. I am learning to heal.

LIFE IS BEAUTIFUL

After gloria died, I found random letters she had written to me. I found them in her house, in my apartment, and in old books; they were everywhere. I also found her journals. In one entry it was there. Right there! An entry in which she wrote "danyelle," with a "y" and all lowercase...always. I learned that I was named while she was sitting in a prison cell. Imprisoned with other women she had known since she had run away from home, gloria wrote that I would be better than she was. I was her first daughter, and she got that right. I would be better than the circumstances into which I was being born. My name would be one that people knew. Women who were whole and healthy would care for me in ways that she had never learned how. I would be guided and protected by women who knew how to mother little Black girls. I would not be overlooked.

In reflection, the rungs in the ladder of my life were only tightly secured by strong women, many of them

Black, who *chose* to love me. With each step that I took, it was their hand that I stepped into. They led me with their hearts and guided me into becoming the woman, mother, and wife that I am today. My mother ignited that spark. My mother had a plan for my life. She had hopes for me, though she lacked execution. It took her death for my realization.

Accepting gloria for who she was—a woman with mental health issues and her own trauma that I could never understand until I examined my own—was vital to my healing process. It was a harsh realization that I had been born into a failed system with no real hope of rescue. Taking the time to explore my life, the themes that carried their way into my adulthood, my pain, and my circumstances ignited a fire to be different, not just for me but for my own daughters. Chains needed to be broken. Curses needed to be destroyed. I learned forgiveness.

Early in my life, I knew that I always wanted to work with children. I wanted to be a beacon for children who were disadvantaged. Looking back, I realize this innate need to care and protect children came from the loss I felt as a young girl. This passion gave me a much-needed purpose as I began to navigate a new, unchartered journey.

Self-love was the first step. This is who I am, scars and all. I learned how to own every one of them. I learned and I grew with every single heartbreak and disappointment. As I believed that I was a product of my circumstances, I thought that I would be just like gloria when I grew up. How could I not? Without appropriate modeling, I had no concept of how my life could differ. Planning was essential in breaking this mold. What steps would I take to change course? Could I navigate this journey with grace and dignity? These were questions that I asked myself and came to expect from the people who surrounded me. If someone could not help me navigate into a fruitful and positive space, there was no room for them in my life and the lives of my children. I deliberately cultivated a healthy support system that encourages me and pushes me to persevere. My "family" are people who choose to love me even if they are not related to me by blood. I've learned how to love God and how to find beauty in my world every single day. I've learned how to practice gratitude and how to give to others wholeheartedly. I finished school and then kept going. I traveled so that I could meet different people and study different cultures. I boldly made those decisions because I found value in myself. I've created new themes—self-reflection, planning, navigating, and conquering. I am still a work in progress but am grateful for the wherewithal to withstand life's storms and the ability to persevere. I am learning to conquer.

Afterword

The journey, the stories shared in these pages, should provide hope and encouragement that no matter your life experience, you can not only survive but also find life, love, joy, and happiness after the darkness. These women have authentically shared their experiences to let you know that you can too rise beyond any situation. We fall down but find victory in standing up, picking up the pieces, and moving on. As the Bible says, "joy cometh in the morning" (Psalm 30:5).

Tasha, the "Champion" after the storm, after the pain, hurt, struggle, and tears is not only *still* standing, she is running the race of life in great form. Tasha found her voice and turned her pain into purpose. With her light shining brightly, she stayed the course. Her past suffering has enabled her to bring life, encouragement, and strength to many. From the cancer patients she has counseled and supported through their darkest moments to the words of wisdom she drops on "Tasha Tuesday," Tasha has showed incredible strength fighting breast cancer while raising four children alone without complaint. In fact, she made it look easy, making speeches and bringing awareness to the importance of breast examination and BRCA testing. She wore that shaved head like a warrior with a vivacious smile. There was never a pity party. Her positive energy, faith in God, and spiritual consciousness are transparent.

Her visions are becoming her reality. Tasha is no longer the frightened little girl trying to fit in; she is blazing her own trail and has truly become a SHEnomenal woman. I am so very proud of her strength, resilience, tenacity, and willingness to evolve. As we continue this journey together, I will be cheering, praying, and supporting her. Congratulations, and thank you for sharing your story and providing a platform for other women to share their story.

Love you dearly,
Valerie Curry
Affectionately known as Auntie Val

About the Authors

Ann-Marie Anderson was born in St. Vincent & the Grenadines and moved to the United States at the age of eight. The oldest of six children, she was a sister mom to her siblings while her mom finished her degree. An athlete and scholar in high school, she went on to study Business Administration and Accounting. She has worked in that field for over 20 years. She's a mom of three children—two daughters and a son. Her desire is to empower women to live life on their terms without regret and shame. She hopes to one day develop an organization that will help train and equip women to realize their full potential.

To connect, email her at
annmariean@gmail.com

Bianca A. Page, JD, is a licensed and ordained minister, soul developer, and spiritual and relationship coach. Bianca was raised in the Spiritual Israel Church, where she currently serves on several auxiliaries. A talent development manager, an attorney at a major law firm, and a graduate of UCLA, Loyola Law School (Los Angeles), and the Israel Spiritual School of Theology, she has served on boards for both philanthropic and spiritual growth purposes. She co-founded The C.O.R.E of U—Community of Restoration and Enlightenment—inspiring individuals to develop self-awareness and transformational practices.

Raised in a loving home, Bianca realized how essential self-love and personal development are to navigate through life. She is a prayer warrior who enjoys touching other souls through speaking and writing, and has a passion to help humankind find peace and joy during their earth journey with an emphasis on coaching women and youth. Her biggest joy comes from being a mother and wife.

Learn more at
www.thecoreofu.com

Camille Telicia (Tuh-lee-see-ya), MBA, is a transforma-tional success coach based in Atlanta, Georgia, and the founder of The Intentional Goddess, a company dedicat-ed to supporting women leaders and entrepreneurs on their journey of self-expansion. She is passionate about empowering women to Know, Love, and Trust them-selves fully and deeply so they can confidently embrace their goddess power and create lives and businesses that change the world. She offers coaching, programs, work-shops, and events curated especially for powerful women to heal and grow.

Camille is the author of *Shut the Stuff Up*, a per-sonal development book designed to help readers shut down the fears, false stories, and limiting beliefs holding them hostage from their goals. She is also the host of the iGoddessTings Podcast, a show for women about life, spirituality, growth, and everything in between.

Camille is a graduate of the University of Georgia (BS, Psychology) and the Florida Institute of Technology (MBA, Business Management).

Learn more at
www.theintentionalgoddess.com

Carol Swanson-Carr was born and raised in British Columbia, Canada and immigrated to the USA in 1986. Carol received a degree in Design and Marketing. These skills allowed her to travel with the company for which she worked to open a design store in several cities in Canada. That led her to Southern California to do the same. She was married and raised two children in the Mojave Desert. While the years passed, she spent countless hours volunteering within her community. Growing up, she was taught to lead by example and taught her children the importance of being involved where you live. She also taught them to not complain unless they were willing to do something about it. Carol continues to live in Southern California and enjoys spending time with her children and grandchildren. She works, volunteers, and continues to be a positive influence with her community.

To connect, email her at
cjswansoncarr@gmail.com

Danisha Jeter, RN-BSN is a wife, mother of four, registered nurse, and co-owner of TNT Photo Booth and Dirdy Deedz Dumping. She was born and raised in Los Angeles, California where she attended and graduated from Crenshaw High School in 1997. She had her first child at the age of 17 and seeing firsthand the difficulties of single parenthood from her own mother, with whom she had a complicated relationship, she was determined to avoid those same pitfalls. The relationship with her children's father grew quite tumultuous, but despite her relationship difficulties, she pushed through her educational goals and in 2013 graduated magna cum laude from Brandman University with a bachelor's degree in nursing and a certificate in Public Health. Danisha has settled in her career and is currently employed with Infusion Partners. She has been happily married to her husband, Trevis Jeter since 2014.

To connect, email her at
nursejeter1@gmail.com

Erin Kelly is a daughter, sister, and loyal friend born and raised in the South Central part of Los Angeles. Wanting to be in a service-based industry, Erin stepped out on faith and traded over 15 years of sitting at a desk in corporate America for a dream in the sky with a new career as a flight attendant, based out of Atlanta, Georgia, where she currently resides. She has a passion for interior design and loves to volunteer in community events that benefit the well being of less fortunate people.

As an author, Erin has chosen to reveal an undiscussed part of her life as part of her personal healing. She wants people to know domestic violence comes in multiple forms and the strength to walk away and forgive reestablishes and increases your personal power.

To connect, email her at
erinkelly81@gmail.com

Janise Salonga-Warner is a mother of four awesome children, has a loving husband of 20 years and recently welcomed her first granddaughter. Her passion for helping and caring for others drove her to obtain an Associates in Healthcare Administration. She recently celebrated her 18th year of working as a registered medical assistant. Janise often gives back to the community by donating clothing, food, and various items to the same cooperative ministries from which her family obtained assistance in years past. Simple pleasures such as visiting a nearby beach or staying at a hotel on long weekends with the family help ease the stress of everyday life. Having lost her parents as a young girl, Janise never thought the life she lives now was what God had in store for her. Staying spiritually connected to God is one main way she keeps herself grounded.

To connect, email her at
janisesalonga@gmail.com

Kiana "Vi" Ware is a project manager by day and the CEO of a full-service design company by night. Priding herself in versatility, she has over eight years of experience leading projects in the commercial, private, and government sectors as well as 10 years of experience as a graphic artist and CEO. Although she loves the purpose her daily grind brings, her true desire is to quit her 9-5 to become a full-time entrepreneur. Vi has been featured in several published works for her illustrations and has commissioned countless logo designs, custom canvases, and murals.

Learn more at
www.bewaredesigns.com/story

LaToya Elliott is every woman. Wife. Mother. Woman of Faith. Her parents and sisters set forth clear ideals and instilled in LaToya a mission not only to succeed but to serve. She was surrounded by strong influences growing up, which is evidenced in both her professional accomplishments and her enduring spirit. Success led the once aspiring lawyer to earn degrees from the University of Michigan and Walsh College. Years later, LaToya leveraged her business acumen and entrepreneurial expertise to create Events by Elliott, LLC, a full-service event management company. She is also the founder of the Key of David Worship Arts Camp. LaToya's mission is to live her life utilizing her God-given gifts and talents to serve, encourage, and show love to others. Her here and now is a culmination of the wisdom and support from her family, an unwavering trust in God, and her undeniable desire to glorify Him.

To connect, email her at
latoya@keyofdavidcamp.com

Lawana Hall-Conklin is a native of Los Angeles, California, a single mother of three, a senior business administrator for a manufacturing consulting firm, owner and cake artist at Word of Mouth Sweets and Treats, and a breast cancer survivor. Lawana earned her BA from Grambling State University in Mass Communications with a concentration in Public Relations. She has been a contributing writer for *Grooveline*, a magazine that represents southern hip hop and HBCU life and *LSQ*, a municipal marijuana publication. Since her encounter with breast cancer, Lawana has become an advocate for cancer warriors and survivors and their caregivers. She and her sons support Celebrate Life Cancer Ministries and Walk 3 to 9. Both organizations work to raise money, awareness, and resources for cancer patients. In 2019, Lawana was presented the Survivor Award from Still I Rise From Cancer, Inc.

To connect, email her at
wordofmouthgs@gmail.com

Mina London is an entrepreneur, wife, and author, but her proudest accomplishment is being a mother to her two precious children. In 2020, Mina launched a lifestyle blog, *Love, Health, & Beyond* where she interviews aspiring business owners while also writing and sharing different lifestyle guides to living a healthier cleaner life. Mina enjoys writing poetry and songs when she is not blogging or writing books. She is dedicated to turning her negative life experiences into positives by sharing her walks of life. She hopes to inspire people to recognize how life is all about moving forward in honesty and truth, making yourself a priority, accepting changes, and looking forward to what makes you stronger and more complete.

Learn more at
www.lovehealthbeyond.com

Mka Morris is an advocate for equality, self-love, and women's empowerment. Her messages are intentional and encourage you to live a power-packed and meaningful life on purpose. Mka is a dedicated wife and mother. She devotes her time to motivating women to seek clarity, tap into their personal truth, and visualize a long-term plan to create their own place in the world.

Mka understands that life teaches you lessons that no one else can. She has mastered the art of manifesting an ideal life through prayer, faith, and positive thinking. Her words will push you to do the same while fostering an apology free lifestyle without limits. You can find her live weekly on Instagram, co-hosting @theaprilandtomeekashow

To connect, email her at
brizaiah326@gmail.com

Nicole Curry is a lupus warrior who has made it her mission to bring awareness to invisible illnesses and otherwise hidden disabilities. She is the founder of the Sistas of Strength (S.O.S.) online support community. Her primary goal is to offer support to other lupus warriors and educate their families, friends, and loved ones by giving them a glimpse into the everyday lives of the 'autoimmuner' through a raw and unfiltered lens. Nicole is a graduate of CSULB's Department of Biological Sciences. Being very community service oriented, she remains diligent in her service as a youth and young adult mentor/advocate, which has also been her passion for 20+ years. She served as a member of the Board of Directors for The Men's Cancer Network. Inc. and The Be Good to Women Collective until her health would no longer permit.

To connect, email her at
nicoleacurry77@gmail.com

Pamela Lathan is an entrepreneur and former co-owner of Mz Lynn's Day Spa & Salon; a HR consultant with a focus on organizational development and virtual professional development training; and COO of Workplace Chaplain Services. Pamela has a Master's Degree in Human Resource Management and 20+ years of HR experience in Corporate America. Pamela is also a lifelong member of the Spiritual Israel Church & Its Army and wears many hats in the organization. She is a 30-year ordained Bride Mother and former First Lady & Co-Founder/Director of the organization's Youth Outreach Program.

Born and raised in New York City, Pamela is now vibrating higher with her husband of 18 years on the West Coast in sunny California. The transition to California was emotional leaving behind her elderly mom and other family members, but once there, things have worked out for all, and now she can journey on living her best life!

To connect, email her at
mslynn1030@gmail.com

Regina Weatherspoon-Bell is a wife, mom, daughter, sister, businesswoman, nonprofit founder/CEO, creative event and documentary producer, and community volunteer. Over the past eight years Regina served as Deputy Director for the First District San Bernardino County Supervisor. During the past twelve years, she's guided her nonprofit, Dreamers, Visionaries & Leaders (DVL) Project, to become a well-known established brand providing cultural enrichment programs and scholarships throughout the High Desert. She serves on several boards, including Providence Health Care Regional Board and High Desert Community Foundation. She remains an advisor to the CEO of Lil Mogul Holdings, owned by notable actress, director, and producer, Kim Fields.

Regina *is the recipient of several honors and recognitions for her work and community service.* In her own words, "It's a blessing, honor and privilege to serve!"

Learn more at
www.dvlproject.com

Saraileah Cassanova is a loving mother who serves on the African American Parent Advisory Counsel at her son's school. She is an autism advocate and, due to previous experience, an advocate for suicide awareness and domestic violence prevention. Living with the autoimmune disease, lupus, Leah lives a healthy, active lifestyle while practicing holistic healing like prayer, journaling, meditation, and yoga.

She currently operates a home-based business providing security consulting services for small businesses and major corporations. Saraileah, having a creatively talented spirit, will be relaunching her women's underclothes line, Cotton Kandies. With the hope of showing the world how children with autism can become productive independent adults, she is starting a nonprofit organization for parents with children of autism. Her upcoming book will detail her accounts of anxiety, depression, and childhood trauma and how she endured through the most devastating day of her life.

To connect, email her at
SaraileahCassanova@gmail.com

Seante Glass-Flowers is an executive chef and owner of Enchanté's Catering. She graduated summa cum laude from culinary arts school and has received numerous write-ups in the *Los Angeles Beat Magazine*. She also catered events for rapper Rick Ross during the 2011 NBA All-Star Weekend. However, she finds her best pleasure preparing unique and exquisite dishes for small gatherings and intimate parties for her personal clients.

Her professional journey has evolved from a chef to a business owner, and now to an author. The mother of three is now using her life experiences to help tell her story. When asked what motivates her to share her story, she states that her goal is to give hope to the hopeless and to inspire people to keep moving forward and never give up on their dreams and aspirations.

To connect, email her at
chefseanteflowers@icloud.com

Sherri Pickett's most fulfilling and challenging experience has been raising her seven children as a single mother. Although she has a BS in Computer Information Systems, she has chosen to work in the field of education. She has taught for 14 years in a variety of roles. She has been involved in church as a Sunday school teacher and a youth director. Writing has been a passion since she began entering writing contests in the fourth grade. She recently became a published author in *The Upper Room*. She is also a three-year breast cancer survivor.

To connect, email her at
kpic6@yahoo.com

Shirrell F. Edey, MBA, is an aspiring author, world traveler, business owner, and entrepreneur. She earned her MBA with minors in Human Resource Management and Communications. She is currently owner and Executive Chef at L.O.V.E (Living Our Vision Everyday) Premier Catering & Events and franchise owner of Chefs for Seniors ~ LA South Bay with a mission to expand personal chef services for seniors in need. Shirrell also doubles as a certified travel agent to fuel her passion to see the world. She volunteers, walks, and participates in fundraisers for the American Heart Association, Susan G. Komen Cancer Foundation, Alzheimer's Association, and AIDS Project Los Angeles.

Shirrell has a testimony of being a phoenix, which she will share in her upcoming autobiography detailing her journey "home." She hopes to touch and encourage anyone who feels they have lost their way to living their true potential.

Learn more at
www.lovepremierevents.com

Shonta' Taylor is an Evangelist who intentionally lives her life with purpose. She is the mother of two amazing sons, DuChein and Cortlin, and a beautiful daughter, Jhai. After living years in the fast life, Shonta never imagined her life would be where it is today. Determined to make a change, she embarked on a journey of healing.

Shonta' will be detailing her life's journey from surviving to thriving in an upcoming book. She credits building her relationship with God as what got her through being preyed on as a child and kidnapped by a pedophile that left her feeling broken, worthless, and unloved to building a relationship with God.

She's passionate about encouraging people to build a relationship with God. Her testimony has given her a platform to serve various outreach programs and oversee multiple ministry auxiliaries.

She lives by the quote, "Be the change you wish to see in the world" by Mahatma Gandhi.

To connect, email her at
missyshontataylor@gmail.com

Tasha Champion is a certified master life coach, intuitive healer, and award-nominated bestselling author. Healing from her personal struggles, she launched Champion EmpowHERment, which specializes in supporting women through self-love and discovering their purpose. Her goal is to heal the very parts of women that used to leave her in tears.

Selected as a Voices of Hope Honoree in 2018 with the American Cancer Society, Tasha consistently speaks to raise awareness and funding to eradicate cancer. Through her experience as a breast cancer survivor, she also works with families affected by cancer, helping them live through the diagnosis and treatment.

Her positive attitude, mindset, energy, and strong love for God and the faith He instilled in her is why she has been able to overcome many obstacles. She continues to use her experience to reach other women and empower them to love the champion they are.

Learn more at
www.shenomenal.com

Theresa D. Polley-Shellcroft, MA, Fine Arts, was born and raised in Huntington, West Virginia. With a passion for expression through the visual arts, she holds a Bachelor of Science in Art Education and a Master of Art in Fine Arts and has continued post-graduate studies in Art History, African Students, and African American Studies. Community dedicated, in 2004, she founded *tps Creative Expressions, Inc.*, a 501(c)(3) organization that promotes the arts in the community and fosters creativity, appreciation, and awareness of the value of arts. Her personal artworks have been exhibited in galleries and museums around the country. She has worked in private and public collections, including the Afro American Museum of History and Culture, Wilberforce, Ohio and the Anacostia Museum of African American History and Culture, Smithsonian Institution, Washington, DC. In addition to fostering her own creative expression, she is dedicated to the fostering of creative expression in others.

To connect, email her at
theresa.shellcroft@gmail.com

danyelle s. goitia beal, MA, BCBA, is a PsyD candidate who's currently completing her dissertation regarding resiliency in Black American women. danyelle holds degrees in Child Development/Psychology and in Teaching (Deaf & Hard of Hearing)/Applied Behavior Analysis. After discovering she was pregnant, losing her mother, and adopting her little brother all within the first year of college, danyelle began a journey of self-healing. She has a passion for children diagnosed with developmental/psychological disorders. She also has a heart for Black girls/women who struggle with finding themselves.

danyelle currently operates an NPA called Loving Hands FSS. She's married to her high school sweetheart, Trevor, and has two beautiful daughters, Alyxia Monae & Skylar Rose. danyelle considers God and her family as the catalyst to everything she does.

To connect, email her at
danyelle.beal@lovinghandsca.com

CREATING DISTINCTIVE BOOKS
WITH INTENTIONAL RESULTS

We're a collaborative group of creative masterminds
with a mission to produce high-quality books to position
you for monumental success in the marketplace.

Our professional team of writers, editors, designers,
and marketing strategists work closely together to ensure
that every detail of your book is a clear representation
of the message in your writing.

Want to know more?
Write to us at info@publishyourgift.com
or call (888) 949-6228

Discover great books, exclusive offers, and more at
www.PublishYourGift.com

Connect with us on social media

@publishyourgift

CPSIA information can be obtained
at www.ICGtesting.com
Printed in the USA
LVHW051536100621
689905LV00009B/883